"A must read for anyone working with young people! Our effectiveness as educators requires that we consider the inner life of students. Anyone who has gone through the traditional educational system will relate to this book."

Alison Medeck, School Counselor
Forestview Middle School
Baxter, Minnesota

"This book is an amazing visual journey that enables readers to reflect on their experiences playing the roles of Little Red Riding Hood, grandmother, the woodsmen and even the wolf. Thank you for inspiring teachers to recognize the wolf and join the woodmen's team to empower all learners to embrace the Little Red Riding Hood inside and find and celebrate their true self."

Kathy Berry, Vice President
Strategic Learning Initiatives
Chicago, Illinois

"American education is often much more a cautionary tale than a fairy tale with a happy ending. Paul invites educators to think critically about their practice in these changing times and encourages those of us in the classroom to focus on people, not programs, to ignite the fires of curiosity again. In doing so he helps us create a happier ending for every stakeholder. Every administrator, counselor, and teacher should read this book. Let the conversation begin!"

Adam Gaff, Spanish Teacher
Center Grove High School
Greenwood, Indiana

"This inspiring book clearly shows that teachers need to create an emotionally safe environment. Paul Bernabei provides countless strategies which foster student engagement. The essential message to the students is: 'You matter.'"

Delaine Moe, Student Assistance Coordinator
Racine Unified School District
Racine, Wisconsin

First printing

ISBN 978-0-692-22436-6

Top 20 Publishing
1873 Stanford Avenue
St. Paul, Minnesota
Phone: 651-308-4876
E-mail: info@top20training.com
Web: www.top20training.com

Other Books Authored by Paul Bernabei

Top 20 Students: Discovering the Best-kept Thinking, Learning and Communicating Secrets of Successful Teenagers

Top 20 Teachers: The Revolution in American Education

Top 20 Parents: Raising Happy, Responsible and Emotionally Healthy Children

Top 20 TLC Teacher's Manual for Grades 3-6

Top 20 Teens Teacher's Manual for Grades 7-12

Why Students Disengage in American Schools

and What We Can Do About It

Paul Bernabei
with Kevin Brennan

Illustrations by Tim Parlin

CONTENTS

FOREWARD

Pursuing Unanswerable Questions in Good Company

My friend Suzy Riley knows my passion for trying to understand the experiences students have in school and the impact those experiences have on their learning and lives. She recently sent me this quote by Rachel Naomi Remen:

> **"Perhaps the secret of living well is not in having all the answers but in pursuing unanswerable questions in good company."**

Throughout my life journey, I have always been in good company. My parents, grandparents and family members have made countless sacrifices for my wellbeing. My wife Paula, our daughters Megan, Molly, Katie and Maripat, their spouses and children, and my extended in-laws have created a family of belonging and acceptance that models appreciation for the uniqueness and worth of each person. Friends and work associates have been people with whom I have enjoyed relaxing play, serious conversations and creative endeavors. They have been models of people who live a purposeful life dedicated to service to others. My dear business partners, Tom Cody, Willow Sweeney, Mary Cole, and Michael Cole, have developed Top 20 Training into a company that makes a significant difference in the lives of thousands of students, parents, educators and other adults. To the extent that I have lived well, it is because of these people. I have been in good company.

Significant among my good company have been teachers. I use that word for anyone who works with or services students of any age: classroom teachers, administrators, coaches, counselors, aids, maintenance and office staff, cooks, bus drivers and many more. I cherish and respect the people I have come to know in my profession: my teachers when I was a student, teachers who were my colleagues during my 28 years in schools, and 350,000 teachers who have attended Top 20 Training sessions because they wanted to make a positive difference in the lives of their students. My teachers include numerous authors of fiction and nonfiction whose books have enriched my life by enabling me to see beyond my limited vision.

I have also been in the good company of young people who I have enjoyed the privilege of teaching, counseling and coaching. I am certain that I have learned more from them than they have from me. They have been a constant reminder that I do not have all the answers and need to keep searching.

Throughout the book, I will frequently use the phrases Top 20 and Bottom 80. I intend these phrases to relate specifically to effectiveness. Top 20 will mean that we are being effective in how we think, learn or communicate and Bottom 80 will mean that we are not being effective in how we think, learn or communicate. In whatever role we are experiencing (student, parent, teacher, coach, friend, employer/employee), there are times when we are being effective (Top 20) and times when we are being ineffective (Bottom 80).

These phrases are not intended to compare one person to another or one group to another. They simply refer to two dimensions that we have, times when we are effective and times when we are not. In that sense, we are all Top 20s and Bottom 80s.

It is a blessing in life to be able to work with people whom we admire and enjoy. For me, that blessing is personified in my partners, Tom Cody, Willow Sweeney and Kevin Brennan.

Tom has been a math teacher for 40 years. We met over 20 years ago as opposing basketball coaches. He invited me to participate in a class he was beginning to teach at Cretin-Derham Hall High School in St. Paul, Minnesota. The class is called TLC (Thinking, Learning and Communicating). This class and our relationship with Mary and Michael Cole became the foundation of our Top 20 Training company and its mission to help people become more effective and develop their potential. Tom is an incredible teacher who has gone through his own personal and professional transformation towards living more as a Top 20. He is bright, quick-witted, outrageously organized, and dedicated to his students. He is especially concerned about students who experience greater social and emotional challenges in school. Tom and his wife Judy have three sons and live in St. Paul.

Born in a hippy commune in Virginia, Willow is unique. She taught social studies at Cretin-Derham Hall High School for eight years. She partnered with Tom in teaching the TLC class, and they became a dynamite team. She now splits her time as a stay-at-home mother or by facilitating unforgettable Top 20 Training sessions. Willow says she travels around the country with two old men (Tom and me). She is funny, compassionate, generous and engaging. She connects with people, remembers their names and goes the extra mile for others. Willow believes the ideal woman would be a mixture of Carol Burnett and Dolly Parton. She's all that plus a lot of Mother Teresa. Willow and her husband Brian have two sons and live in St. Cloud, Minnesota.

Although 30 years younger than I, Kevin Brennan is my mentor. Kevin has been a high school English teacher for ten years. Every student I meet who has had Mr. Brennan in class smiles when they talk about that experience. Now that he is no longer in the classroom and is doing trainings for our Top 20 company, I get the same response from teachers and parents who have attended his sessions. Kevin is dedicated to his family, faith, and our Top 20 mission…to transform American education so that students and teachers experience incredible learning, abundant enjoyment and meaningful personal development during their time in schools. In coauthoring this book with me, Kevin has brought his skill, passion and deep concern for the well being of students, educators, and our profession. Kevin and his wife Gina live in St. Paul, Minnesota, with their daughter and three sons.

I will frequently reference my partners in the book as Tom, Willow, and Kevin.

I want to thank friends and colleagues who read drafts of this book and provided valuable feedback. I am especially grateful to Maribeth

Mohan who spent several days teaching me how to write using the English language and making this book readable.

Throughout the book I will alternate gender references with the pronouns he and she.

Paul Bernabei
St. Paul, Minnesota
May 2014

DEDICATION

For 13 years I have been in the very good company of 13 grandchildren who are each unique and special to me and represent young people throughout the world who dream about becoming their true selves. They have revealed to me the delightful and tender inner life of children, have shown me what children need, and have manifested in their lives the potential that develops when those needs are met. I am grateful to them for being their grandfather's teacher. They and the young people they represent motivate me to pursue unanswerable questions.

I dedicate this book to my grandchildren in the order by which they became my greatest teachers:

Jack Fenlon	Joe Fenlon	Matthew Giefer
Caroline Fenlon	Joe Haughey	Isla Giefer
Emily Fenlon	Charlie Fenlon	Emma Fenlon
Maggie Fenlon	Ellie Haughey	
Kate Haughey	Matthew Fenlon	

(A note about the eight Fenlon children on this list: two of our daughters married Fenlon brothers. The first four Fenlon children belong to our daughter Molly and the second four belong to our daughter Katie.)

INTRODUCTION

History is the experience of a people from the past to the present. Our history is the story of how we got from there to here. It is the story of what we did and what happened to us along the way. It is the story of our life...the values we've held dear, the decisions we've made, the actions we've taken. It is what has gone on inside us...our thoughts, feelings and beliefs...and what's gone on outside us as we have engaged with the world and other people. Our history is significant for each person individually and for us as a people living in America in the 21st century.

One reason why history is critically important is that it includes those experiences and events that have formed us, the experiences and events that have helped us develop our potential as human beings and those that have blocked or deterred our development. Certainly one of the most powerful forces that has formed us and impacted the development of our potential is our education...our experience

Potential: a power within us that waits, waits, waits to get activated so it can come through us to make a positive difference in the quality of our lives, relationships and experiences.

of learning. What has that experience been in our history and what do we want that experience to be in our future? That's a profound question that needs serious consideration. What young people are experiencing in their formal education is significant in their lives, and in turn, in our life as a people as we actively write our history each day.

The purpose of this book is to pursue some questions that are not completely answerable about how students experience school. At times in this book I might sound like I have all the answers. I do not. However, I do want to give these questions some serious thought from my own very limited perspective and from what I have learned by listening for nearly 50 years to countless students, educators, par-

1

ents and other concerned adults. In addition, I would like this book to engage you to identify and acknowledge your perspective on these questions and to contribute that perspective to the dialogue on how we can best use education for the development of our youth and the enrichment of our future. In the good company of each other, I believe we can discover better answers. We will not come up with complete answers, but we can discover answers that will matter to the students we teach and serve.

"(T)he only way to get out of trouble," contends Parker Palmer, "is to go deeper in. We must enter, not evade, the tangles of teaching so we can understand them better and negotiate them with more grace, not only to guard our own spirits but also to serve our students well."[1]

The questions I am most concerned about have to do with what is causing students to disengage in school. "In the United States," according to Alliance for Excellent Education, "an average of 30 percent of students who enter the 9th grade in school will dropout before the 12th grade and not graduate from high school. In some areas the proportion is as high as 50 percent. In some Native American communities it's over 80 percent. Among those who stay the course, rates of underachievement and disaffection are often desperately high."

In his book *Out of Our Minds,* Ken Robinson argues, "It's wrong to blame the students for these numbers: they reflect a problem within the system. Any other standardized process with a 30 percent wastage rate, let alone 50 percent or 80 percent, would be condemned as a failure. In the case of education it isn't a waste of inert commodities; it's a waste of living, breathing people."[2]

James Marshall Crotty, in his article titled "Motivation Matters: 40% Of High School Students Chronically Disengaged From School," references a series of papers released by the Center on Education Policy (CEP) at the George Washington University. The CEP papers suggest "that while existing efforts to increase student achievement are an important part of education reform, they have not focused enough on what it takes to motivate students in school. Too often, strategies that adults use to boost student achievement — such as raising academic standards and giving high-stakes standardized exams — do not address the real reasons why students are disengaged."[3] The purpose of this book is to focus on the real reasons why students are disengaged and how we as their teachers can help them maintain their motivation for learning.

Student disengagement includes students who are truant or drop out of school. These students are easy to detect. Disengagement also includes students who attend school on a daily basis but are tardy for class, sleep during class, find school boring or irrelevant, or who sit quietly and appear to be paying attention but have mentally drifted off to their own world outside of school. The hardest group to detect includes students who have learned how to play the game. These are the students who take notes, do their homework, ask questions in class, get help from their teachers, study for tests and get good grades. However, in learning how to play the game and get good grades, they have lost their passion and desire for learning.

The problem is not that our students experience moments of disengagement. Moments of daydreaming or being distracted are not the concern of this book. The problem for our students and for their future occurs when disengagement becomes a habit. The habit of disengagement can impact our students well beyond their school experience. A Gallup study published in 2001 estimates that 'actively disengaged employees' were costing the US economy between $292 and $355 billion a year.[4]

Engaged students, quite simply, have a passion for learning. They are rare in American schools. Why is that? Why do students disengage from school in the various ways mentioned above?

The Big Question I want to pursue in this book is: **Why do students lose their passion for learning and disengage in American schools?**

Before pursuing this question, let's identify four questions that will guide our search for meaningful, although incomplete, answers to the Big Question.

- Although education is a constant experience in the lives of human beings, the purpose of this book is to focus on formal education and, particularly, formal education between kindergarten and senior year in high school. What do students really experience during these 13 years of school?

- What impact does what they experience have on their inner lives?

- Does their experience cause the unintended consequence of disengaging from school and learning?

- What can we do to minimize student disengagement and help them maintain their natural desire to learn?

Thoughts about the Big Question and these four guiding questions will be woven throughout four parts of this book.

Part 1: A Place Called School focuses on how students experience school. It introduces the story of Little Red Riding Hood as a backdrop for what school is like for many students in American schools in the 21st century.

Part 2: The Inner Life of Students examines how the messages that students receive form powerful beliefs that impact student engagement or disengagement.

Part 3: Engagement 101 considers ways we can maintain student engagement by creating a culture of learning.

Inner Life: a person's true self that embodies her identity, worth and purpose and includes her mental, emotional and spiritual life, potential, and creativity.

Part 4: It's Possible includes examples of a class and a school where student disengagement is being intentionally addressed.

Thanks for being good company as we pursue these unanswerable questions in an effort to better serve the young people we teach and parent and help them develop the incredible potential residing in each of them.

PART 1

A Place Called School

CHAPTER ONE

Little Red Riding Hood Goes to School

For many of us stories have been a source of learning and enjoyment throughout our lives. Parents use stories to engage, calm, and enlighten their children; families share stories of relatives from previous generations; English teachers use books to help their students understand human nature; social studies and history teachers use stories to transport their students to past lives and eras to ensure understanding; math teachers use mini stories to simulate logical problem solving.

One of the most loved and popular stories of all time is the fairy tale of Little Red Riding Hood. Over the years the story of a young girl going to visit her grandmother has been adapted numerous times for various intents and purposes.

We will use this classical story as a metaphor for what students experience in school. Elements of this simple children's story can be compared to the many moments of confidence and fear, or engagement and disengagement, which students experience in school on a day-to-day basis.

The following is an adaptation of the Brothers Grimm's version of Little Red Riding Hood.[1]

> Once upon a time there was a dear little girl who was especially loved by her grandmother. As an expression of her affection, grandmother had given the child a little riding hood of red velvet. Because she wore the red riding hood all the time, the child

came to be called Little Red Riding Hood.

One day Red Riding Hood's mother asked her to bring grandmother a piece of cake and bottle of wine. Undertaking her mother's request, Red Riding Hood excitedly went off by herself for the first time to visit her loving grandmother who lived in the woods half a league from the village. As Red Riding

Hood entered the woods, a wolf met her. Not knowing what a wicked creature he was, Red Riding Hood was not at all afraid of the wolf.

"Good day, Red Riding Hood," he said.

"Good day to you," she said.

"Where are you going so early, Red Riding Hood?"

"To my grandmother's house."

"Where does your grandmother live?" asked the conniving wolf.

"A good quarter of a league farther on in the wood. Her house stands under the three large oak trees," replied Red Riding Hood.

The wolf thought to himself: "What a tender young creature! What a nice plump mouthful! She will be better to eat than the old woman. I must act craftily, so as to catch both."

So he walked with her for a short time and then said: "See, Red Riding Hood, how pretty the flowers are. Why don't you look round? I believe, too, that you do not hear how sweetly the little birds are singing. You walk gravely along as if you were going to school, while everything else out here in the wood is merry."

Red Riding Hood, seeing the sunbeams dancing through the trees and pretty flowers growing everywhere, thought: "Grandmother would be pleased if I brought her some fresh flowers." So she ran from the path into the wood to look for flowers. As she picked one flower, she would see a prettier one further on. She excitedly went deeper and deeper into the woods until she had picked a full bouquet of flowers for Grandmother.

Meanwhile the wolf ran straight to the grandmother's house and knocked at the door.

"Who is there?" Grandmother asked from her bed.

"Little Red Riding Hood," replied the wolf, "bringing you cake and wine. Open the door, Grandmother."

"I am too weak and cannot get up," called out Grandmother. "Lift the latch and come in."

The wolf lifted the latch, entered the house, and, going straight to the Grandmother's bed, devoured her. Then he put on her clothes, dressed himself in her cap, laid himself in bed and drew the curtains.

Red Riding Hood had been running about picking flowers. When she had gathered so many that she could carry no more, she set out on the way to Grandmother's house.

Surprised to find the door open, she had a strange feeling as she entered the cottage: "I like being with Grandmother so much, but I feel uneasy today." Calling out, "Good morning, Grandmother," but receiving no answer, she went to the bed and drew back the curtains. There lay her Grandmother with her cap pulled over her face.

"Put your basket on the table and take off your riding hood," said the wolf.

After doing so, she approached her Grandmother's bed. Seeing how strange her Grandmother looked, Red Riding Hood said, "Oh, Grandmother, what big ears you have!"

"All the better to hear you with, my child."

"But, Grandmother, what big eyes you have!"

"All the better to see you with, my dear."

"But, Grandmother, what large hands you have!"

"All the better to hug you with."

"Oh! Grandmother, what a terrible big mouth you have!"

"All the better to eat you with!"

Scarcely had the wolf said this, when he swallowed up Red Riding Hood.

With his appetite satisfied, the wolf went back to bed, fell asleep and began to snore very loud.

A woodsman was just passing the house and thought to himself: "How the old woman is snoring! I wonder if she needs anything." So he entered the cottage and, seeing the wolf lying in bed, said, "I have long sought you."

About to fire his gun at the wolf, it occurred to him that the wolf might have devoured the Grandmother. Instead, he took a pair of scissors and began to cut open the stomach of the sleeping wolf. When he had made two snips, he saw the little red riding hood shining. After two more snips, the little girl sprang out, crying: "Ah, how frightened I have been! How dark it was inside the wolf."

Then Grandmother, scarcely able to breathe, came out alive also. Red Riding Hood quickly fetched large stones with which they filled the wolf's belly. When he awoke and wanted to run away, the stones were so heavy that he collapsed at once and fell dead.

Grandmother, Red Riding Hood and the woodsman were delighted. But Red Riding Hood thought to herself: "As long as I live, I will never leave the path by myself to run into the wood."

This story is a metaphor for the school experience of students in 21st century America. Little Red Riding Hood represents our students. She is a symbol of the excitement, innocence and curiosity that students often bring when they first enter school. Her questions and willingness to search for flowers remind us of the wonder of students and their natural desire to learn. Her willingness to take off her red riding hood reveals her vulnerability, which is necessary in all learning endeavors.

Grandmother and her cottage represent the joyful experience of belonging where students feel valued, comfortable with their identity, and free to be themselves. The story has Grandmother in bed, showcasing her weak state, indicating that Grandmother is not fully healthy and suggests that there is something dysfunctional in the school experience. Entering Grandmother's cottage and having 'a strange…uneasy' feeling, Red Riding Hood said, "I like being with Grandmother so much, but I feel uneasy today." The little girl senses a threat.

The wolf personifies the threats in school that cause fear. His big eyes and big ears used to size her up and judge her as "a nice plump mouthful" reflect an awareness of all the things that students do in school. His big arms and big mouth indicate the threats experienced in school that overpower students by taking advantage of their innocence and natural curiosity.

Using the wolf as a metaphor for threats that students experience in school can be misleading. In the story of Little Red Riding Hood, the wolf is intentional in wanting to cause her harm. That is rarely the case in school. The threats that cause students to experience fear in school are more commonly the result of unintended consequences. I know that at times as a teacher and administrator I played the role of the wolf. Although never intentional, my practices and communication did appear as a threat and result in my students' reluctance to engage.

After experiencing the threat of the wolf, Red Riding Hood says, "As long as I live, I will never leave the path by myself to run into the wood." The excitement of adventure and the delight of beautiful flowers have been shut down by her fear for survival. As Red Riding Hood's fear is activated, she decides to disengage.

The woodsman represents a teacher who understands the threat and has been on the lookout for it. The woodsman senses subtle changes and takes immediate action to protect and save the students. He restores safety and trust to the school experience. Throughout the book, we will refer to this teacher as a Top 20 teacher, a teacher effective in caring for his students and creating a culture of learning.

As we consider the experience that students have in school, we will apply the characters and elements of this fairy tale. In doing so, we will pose some challenging questions: Can we play the role of the woodsman, revive Grandmother, eliminate the threat of the wolf and encourage Red Riding Hood to safely leave the path to discover the wonders in the woods? Can we minimize fear in school so our students will stay engaged?

Before we pursue these unanswerable questions, we must first look at why students need school and acknowledge the myriad states of mind and being our students are in as they wander down the many paths of school and education.

CHAPTER TWO

Why Do We Need School?

My formal education from grade school (my grade school did not have kindergarten) through high school took place from 1953 to 1965. During those years I had approximately 30 different teachers. Each day, for 12 years, every one of those 30 teachers unscrewed my head and dumped information in. I was a willing student. My head was easy to unscrew. Years later I thank those teachers for what they did. Why? In those days if you got information it came from an encyclopedia or a teacher.

The role of a teacher was to impart information. However, if that is the role of a teacher today, then Google will be the Teacher of the Year. Google will impart more information in one day than a teacher will in her entire career. With that notion in mind, why do we need school if the students can unscrew their own heads and dump Google's information in on their own?

My granddaughter Kate is in first grade. In her first few years of life, her daycare provider was Maria. Maria, who had come from Puerto Rico to Chicago many years ago, was a wonderful nanny for Kate and taught her many Spanish words. When Kate began to speak, she knew as many words in Spanish as she did in English. Why does Kate need school?

When my other grandchildren don't understand something, they pick up their parent's smart phone and Google their questions. The few who are too young to do that will simply say, "Mommy, let's Google that." Within seconds, information is provided. Why do my grandchildren need school?

I met Ed, a 22-year-old waiter, while having dinner with friends at a St. Paul restaurant. Ed seemed bright, articulate and confident as he communicated easily with our group. When I asked Ed where he went to school, he said that he had been home-schooled by his mother. Why does Ed need school?

Coming from an Italian background, I want to visit Italy with my wife in the next few years. To enrich that experience, I would like to know a bit of the Italian language. Since I currently travel quite frequently with my work, I need an Italian teacher who can go where I go. Rosetta Stone has been a perfect teacher for me. She's even available for teaching me when I'm on an airplane. Why do I need school?

What do my grandchildren, Ed and I have in common? We don't need school. If we just want to get information or learn a skill, modern technology and out-of-school opportunities work just fine.

Change Happens

In 1907, the directors of a buggy company came together to assess how their company was doing and determine what their plan should be for the future. Their answer was clear and obvious. Since the company had experienced a tremendously successful year selling buggies, the directors agreed that the company should continue doing what it had been doing. That decision made total sense. However, change was about to happen.

In 1908, Henry Ford's Model T initiated a new era in personal transportation. The Model T, easy to operate, maintain and handle on rough roads, became a huge success. Within a few years the highly successful buggy company was out of business. Change happens.

We can use this story to understand something about education.

A theme in Ken Robinson's book *Out of Our Minds* is our need to conduct our schools in radically different ways. He references Abraham Lincoln's second annual address to Congress in December, 1862: "The dogmas of the quiet past are inadequate to the stormy present....As our case is new, so we must think anew and act new. We must disenthrall ourselves and then we shall save our country."

Robinson explains Lincoln's meaning of the word 'disenthrall' as living "our lives guided by ideas to which we are devoted but which may no longer be true or relevant." Like the directors of the buggy company, we are hypnotized or enthralled by ineffective ideas and "to move forward we have to shake free of them."

Failure to do so will result in our students' inability to discover and develop their natural talents and abilities. "Ironically," claims Robinson, "one of the main reasons for this massive waste of talent is the very process that is meant to develop it: education."

> Current approaches to education and training are hobbled by assumptions about intelligence and creativity that have squandered the talents and stifled the creative confidence of untold numbers of people This waste stems partly from an obsession with certain types of academic ability and from a preoccupation with standardized testing....The waste of talent may not be deliberate but it is systemic...it is based on deep-seated assumptions that are no longer true.[2]

The New Era in Education

According to Webster's Third New International Dictionary, educate is defined as "to provide with information" and education as "the act or process of imparting or acquiring knowledge."[3] If we accept these definitions, then the role of a teacher is to unscrew the heads of students and dump information in.

My friend Dr. David Walsh, who has done wonderful work on the adolescent brain and technology, says we have entered a new era in education. The new era, initiated and driven by computers, smart phones and tablet technologies, has made learning "more, fast, easy, fun." This is what our young people are accustomed to long before they are ready for kindergarten. If information is so readily available, why do we need school?

> "Education is the kindling of a flame, not the filling of a vessel."
>
> — Socrates

The new era in education is asking us to reconsider what education is. The old era, resembling the 1907 buggy company, was valuable for its time. It focused on "imparting or acquiring knowledge." The new era actually derives its focus from a much older root word for education: educere. This Latin word means 'to lead or draw out.' The role of the teacher in the old era was to put something into her students. The role of the teacher in the new era is to draw something out of her students.

Ken Robinson believes that "every child is by nature a unique individual with innate talents and sensibilities. Education should draw out these qualities....Education should not be knowledge-based but child-centered....One of the main roles of teachers is to draw out the individual in every child. In this sense, education is a process of self-realization."[4]

"As we grow up," Robinson continues, "education is meant to guide us from childhood to maturity. It should be high among the ways in which we realize our creative abilities. More often it is why we lose sight of them."[5]

Yes, teachers in the new era will still impart knowledge to their students, but this is no longer their primary or essential function; that is Google's primary purpose. So why do we need school? **We need places where young people meet teachers who create relationships and experiences that activate the potential of students.** Google cannot do that. Teachers can.

> "At the heart of education is the relationship between teachers and students."
>
> —Ken Robinson

The 3 Rs of the old era were reading, writing and arithmetic. (How did we get three Rs out of those?) The 3 Rs of the new era are relationships, realizations and relevancy. When students experience these 3 Rs, their curiosity, the necessary ingredient for engagement and learning, is activated.

3 Rs = Curiousity > Engagement > Learning

The opposite occurs when children experience a negative or unhealthy relationship or do not experience realizations or relevancy. Curiosity takes a hit, disengagement sets in and learning doesn't occur.

Curiosity

Children come with curiosity. It is in them when they are born. Parents or teachers do not put curiosity into children. Parents don't imbue in their children the desire to crawl, walk or build with blocks. Children do these things on their own. Children are naturally curious.

What does curiosity look like? What do we observe when a child is curious? The activity that is manifested by a child's curiosity is 'trying'. Trying is the active expression of a child's curiosity. When children are curious, they engage by trying. When children are curious and try, they learn.

Curiosity > Trying > Learning

The role of a Top 20 teacher in the 21st century is to keep curiosity alive in students. This primary and essential responsibility of a teacher ought to be the first item listed on a teacher's job description: **Keep curiosity alive in students.**

We have gotten a bit off track in our country regarding the purpose of a teacher. The focus seems only to be concerned with outcomes—how

> "Young children enter preschool alive with creative confidence; by the time they leave high school many have lost that confidence entirely."
>
> —Ken Robinson

students perform on tests. We have lost sight of the primary role of the teacher, which is to keep the curiosity of students alive. Curious students will engage in the content and their test scores will reflect this engagement. Students who are no longer curious disengage from learning and their test scores decline.

Teachers in America should be assessed by what happens to their students' curiosity. As a young teacher in the 1970s, I was not focused on my students' curiosity. As I understood it, my job was to dump Shakespeare or grammar or vocabulary words into my students' heads, not foster their curiosity. Unaware of its importance, I often stripped my students of their curiosity. Although that was never intentional, my desire is that no student ever experience this again. Being an effective teacher in the 21st century requires that we keep students' curiosity alive so they will keep trying and stay engaged in learning.

Neglecting the Inner Life of Students

Some years ago, Tom and I were working with 100 middle school students at a character education conference in St. Louis. As we began our session, we asked the students to raise their hands if they believed there was something outside of them that, if they could get it, would improve their lives. Instantly, 100 students raised their hands.

This experience lingered in me for several weeks. It made sense to me that students who lacked essential food, shelter or clothing in their lives would want something outside of them to make their lives better. But the students we were working with were not lacking these basic necessities. Why did they believe so strongly that their lives would be better if they could get something outside of themselves?

One day the answer to that question came to me. They believed it because that's what we have taught them. Our young people are continually sent messages reminding them that they would be happier and more satisfied if they could only get the latest iPhone, the more fashionable shoes, the cuter outfit, the faster computer, the more popular boyfriend or girlfriend, admission to the more prestigious college or university, the higher paying job, the more expensive car, the more luxurious house or the longer vacation. Included in this list would be better grades, higher test scores or a degree.

The frequency of these messages and the glitter by which they are presented shout loud and clear that the quality of our lives is only made possible by **getting** something that comes from outside of ourselves. This philosophy assumes that the quality of our lives has to do with achievement, attainment and accomplishment.

> "To educate is to guide students on an inner journey toward more truthful ways of seeing and being in the world."
>
> —Parker Palmer

Although there is some truth to this, it's not the whole truth. Something is missing. What has been neglected in these messages is attention to our students' inner lives. We need to be more concerned with and help our students become more aware of who they are becoming rather than what they are getting.

Human Being Precedes Human Doing

Joe, my five-year-old grandson, has a sensitive spirit. He's had two school experiences…one year of preschool and one year of kindergarten. After his first month in kindergarten, I asked him how school was going.

"Grampa," Joe said, with bright and excited eyes, "I love school."

"That's great, Joe. Why is that?" I questioned.

"Well last year at the beginning of each day my teacher would say, 'Let's get down to work.'"

His preschool teacher's statement to Joe made total sense to me. Each morning teachers in schools across America call students to get down to work. After all, that's what students come to school to do…to get down to work and learn.

Then Joe said, "But this year my teacher says, 'Hi, Joe, I'm glad you're here.'"

The wisdom of this five-year-old boy reveals a truth that I never realized as a teacher. "Let's get down to work" recognizes my grandson as a **human doer**, but "Hi, Joe, I'm glad you're here" recognizes him as a **human being**. This little boy knows the difference.

Unfortunately, during the time I spent with students in classrooms, I was not aware of that profound and life-changing truth. I saw my students as human doers. As their English and language arts teacher, I wanted my students to **do** reading and **do** writing and **do** grammar and **do** vocabulary. I certainly wanted them to **do** listening and note-taking and **do** studying so they could **do** better in communicating with others and, most importantly, **do** better on tests.

All of this doing was and continues to be essential to what goes on in American schools. Students then and now need to participate and engage in countless doings so they can do learning and do knowing. However, according to Ken Robinson, "Ignoring the human factor is at the root of many of the problems that industrial systems of education have created. Education is not only a preparation for what may come later; it is also about helping people engage with the present. What we become as our lives evolve depends on the quality of our experiences here and now."[6]

What Joe's wisdom reveals to his grandfather is that **doing is the *what* of education, but it is not the *who* or the *why* or the *where* of education.**

> 1. **Who** are these students who come to school?
>
> 2. **Why** are they coming to school?
>
> 3. **Where** are they mentally, emotionally or experientially while they are in school?

Each student enters our schools and classrooms each morning first as a human being. Joe not only knows the difference between human doing and human being, but, put succinctly, his wisdom reveals that **human being precedes human doing.** To neglect this is to threaten and minimize our students' ability to be engaged and successful at human doing.

It is unlikely that a neglected human being will ever become a truly engaged human doer or life-long human learner. Before trying to accomplish the **what** of our students' school experience, we need to focus first on the **who, why** and **where.**

CHAPTER THREE

The Who, Why, and Where of School

Let us look at these questions one more time.

1. Who are these students who come to school?

2. Why are they coming to school?

3. Where are they mentally, emotionally or experientially while they are in school?

These three questions certainly fall into the category of unanswerable. The millions of students who enter American schools each day are tremendously diverse. They are diverse in gender, race, culture, religion, socio-economic background, and family. They are diverse in talent, abilities, disabilities and needs. They are diverse in why they come to school and where they are when they are in school. Yes, unanswerable questions, but essential nonetheless. With this in mind, I'll offer a few very partial answers to these questions, answers that consider the concern about student engagement and disengagement.

Who Is Coming to School: The Inner Life of Students and Their Spirit-to-be

Think of a newborn child. Whenever I see a baby, I imagine within her a unique spirit that has a desire to be and to express herself as she grows and develops through the various stages of life. I refer to this as a person's **spirit-to-be.**

I remember seeing my newborn granddaughter Emily for the first time. As I gazed upon this beautiful child, the words that came to me were: "Emily, you are my beloved granddaughter in whom I am well pleased. Be Emily." I've had a similar experience each time I have seen a grandchild for the first time. Although the name changes, these same fourteen words rush into my consciousness. Upon further reflection, I have come to realize that these words reflect three things about Emily:

- **Identity:** Emily has a unique identity. Her identity is in some way different from every other person who has been born.

- **Worth:** Emily's unique identity has worth and value. Her worth is not based on her **doing** something. It's not based on **what she does,** her achievements or her accomplishments. Rather, it is based solely on her **being.** She has worth and value because of **who she is.**

- **Purpose:** Emily's purpose in her life is to be Emily, to be and express this unique identity throughout her life. Although she can admire and appreciate other people, her purpose is NOT to be others but to be her true self.

Identity, worth and purpose reside uniquely in each person's core. Deep inside each of us we have an instinctive knowing about our unique identity, our worth because of who we are, and our purpose to be our true self. We can think of these as three deeply implanted **original messages** in the DNA of our being. They represent the spirit of each person that instinctively desires to freely express itself. **Each person is a unique spirit-to-be.**

Martha Graham, known as the Picasso of dance and founder of the oldest dance studio in America, stated it this way: "There is a vitality, a life-force, an energy, a quickening that is translated through you into action and because there is only one of you in all of time, this expression is unique. And if you block it, it will never exist through any other medium and be lost."[7]

Made up of these original messages, our spirit-to-be is the North Star by which we are to govern our lives. When we are attuned to these messages and live in accordance with these natural instincts, we experience joy and happiness. We are being who we are intended to be.

Being in the Land of Other People

At the moment of her birth, Emily began a new experience: living on the circumference, or in the Land of Other People. The messages she now receives come from other people. They take the form of Other Peoples' Opinions (OPOs), Other Peoples' Expectations (OPEs), and Other Peoples' Agendas (OPAs). In other words, people tell Emily who she should be and what she should do. These messages come from family members, friends, teachers, the media and countless other sources. They tell Emily how she should think and act, what she should wear, who she should hang out with, what she should like, who she should vote for, what she should buy and on and on and on.

As Emily lives more and more on the circumference and receives more and more messages from the Land of Other People, she will come to believe that her purpose in life is to Please Other People. The message to Please Other People is powerful and effective. It becomes internalized in Emily by her awareness that by pleasing other people they give her things that she likes…a smile or pat on the back, good grades, making the team, an invitation to the party, acceptance into college, a job. It also becomes internalized by her awareness that when she doesn't please other people they give her things that she doesn't like… the 'look', bad grades, not making the team, not getting invited to the party, not getting accepted into college and not getting the job. In the context of these experiences, she will come to believe that her purpose in life is to Please Other People.

As these messages from other people and the importance of pleasing other people get louder and stronger, they drown out the original core messages. Once Emily feels the judgment and comparison that come from other people, once she experiences layer upon layer of other peoples' expectations and opinions, her spirit-to-be will begin to experience fear and threat. As such, instead of her spirit-to-be manifesting itself, it will begin to withdraw. When this occurs, she begins to suffer from amnesia. She will forget her true identity, worth and purpose. The ultimate sadness of this type of amnesia is that it will result in her striving for things, experiences and relationships that will never result in true belonging, joy or happiness.

In various degrees we all suffer from amnesia and forget our three core messages. To the extent that this occurs, our lives are no longer governed by our natural spirit-to-be, but by powerful forces in the outside world. Our worth is determined by what we get, our achievements, accomplishments and attainments, and by the perceived opinions of others. **As we live more and more out of alignment with the truth of who we are, we lose personal power to direct our own lives and are doomed by the judgment of never being good enough.**

The following story illustrates the unique spirit-to-be and what happens to it when messages that come from living on the circumference cause amnesia.

Parable of the Eagle

A certain man went through a forest seeking any bird of interest he might find. He caught a young eagle, brought it home, and put it among his fowls and ducks and turkeys and gave it chickens' food to eat even though it was an eagle, the king of birds.

Five years later a naturalist came to see him and, after passing through his garden, said, "That bird is an eagle, not a chicken."

"Yes," said its owner, "but I have trained it to be a chicken. It is no longer an eagle. It is a chicken even though it measures eight feet from tip to tip of its wings."

"No," said the naturalist, "it is an eagle still; it has the heart of an eagle, and I will make it soar high up to the heavens."

"No," said the owner, "it is a chicken and it will never fly."

They agreed to test it. The naturalist picked up the eagle, held it up, and said with great intensity, "Eagle, you are an eagle; you belong to the sky and not to this earth; stretch forth your wings and fly."

The eagle turned this way and that, and then, looking down, saw the chickens eating their food, and down he jumped.

The owner said, "I told you it was a chicken."

"No," said the naturalist, "it is an eagle. Give it another chance tomorrow."

So the next day he took it to the top of the house and said, "Eagle, you are an eagle; stretch forth your wings and fly." But again the eagle, seeing the chickens feeding, jumped down and fed with them.

Then the owner said, "I told you it was a chicken."

"No," asserted the naturalist, "it is an eagle, and it still has the heart of an eagle; only give it one more chance, and I will make it fly tomorrow."

The next morning he rose early and took the eagle outside the city, away from the houses, to the foot of a high mountain. The sun was just rising, gilding the top of the mountain with gold, and every crag was glistening in the joy of that beautiful morning.

He picked up the eagle and said to it, "Eagle, you are an eagle, you belong to the sky and not to this earth, stretch forth your wings and fly!"

The eagle looked around and trembled as if new life were coming to it. But it did not fly. The naturalist then made it look straight at the sun. Suddenly, it stretched out its wings and, with the screech of an eagle, it mounted higher and higher and never returned. It was an eagle, though it had been kept and tamed as a chicken!

Purpose: Remembering Who We Are

Parker Palmer reminds us that, like the eagle, we are "not victims of external forces but persons possessed with an inner power that cannot be taken from us, though we can and do give it away….(O)ur inner world has a reality and a power that can keep us from being victims of circumstance and compel us to take responsibility for our own lives…. the world of social structures and signals need not dictate our lives."[8]

Fortunately, like the eagle, we sometimes have experiences on the circumference that remind us of who we are at our core. While in the Land of Other People, we sometimes meet someone like the naturalist who sends us a message that reminds us of our spirit-to-be, our worth and purpose. This re-membering, claims Palmer, "involves putting ourselves back together, recovering identity and integrity, reclaiming the wholeness of our lives. When we forget who we are…(we) dis-member ourselves, with unhappy consequences."[9]

My grandfather was an 'uneducated' man.* He came to America from Italy as a teenager in the early 20th century. By the end of his life, he could neither read nor write, including his own name. While growing up in a small town in central Illinois, I spent countless hours with my grandfather walking along the railroad tracks and through the woods to find nuts or berries. I'd watch him in the backyard, as he would step into a large barrel filled with grapes and stomp on them as part of the process of making wine. I would keep score for him and his older Italian friends as they played bocce ball at the local tavern.

Throughout all these times with my grandfather, he always called me 'Mi bocia,' which I understood to mean 'my boy.' My relationship with my grandfather created the space in which my spirit-to-be was free to be. 'Mi bocia' meant that I belonged to him; I was his boy; I had

(*I remember a very educated college professor telling me that once you've been to college you can't stand people who haven't. If that were the case, my college education would mean that I would no longer appreciate my grandfather. What this professor really taught me was that there is a difference between being educated and being wise. I now realize that the wisdom of an 'uneducated' grandfather is of more value than the opinions of an 'educated' professor.)

worth and I was just to be me.

Every student who enters a school comes with worth and a unique spirit-to-be his true self. He also has experienced countless messages on the circumference that have resulted in various degrees of amnesia about his original message. This is 'who' is coming to school, young people who may be experiencing different levels of forgetfulness and dis-membering.

Why Are Students Coming to School?

If students are unique spirits-to-be who have received or will receive messages while living on the circumference that have resulted or will result in amnesia regarding the truth of who they are, 'why' are they coming to school? What do they really need to experience during their time in school?

Let's start with what they don't need to experience. They don't need more messages that contradict the truth of who they are. They don't need more messages that they are chickens; that they are less than who they are. They don't need messages that they need to become someone else in order to have worth or value. They don't need messages that they are not good enough or that they are not smart enough.

Quite simply, what they need is:

    1. To be reminded of who they are at their core.

    2. To discover and develop their potential.

    3. To be able to express the uniqueness of their spirit-to-be.

Peg Diekhoff is the assistant principal at a Native American school. She asked us to spend two days with her senior class of 80 students, half of whom were in danger of not graduating. Peg's dedicated staff works hard to keep students engaged. Nonetheless, for a variety of reasons it is normal for 20 seniors to be absent from school on any particular day. While visiting several classrooms, I frequently observed students asleep or with their heads on the desk. Student disengagement was rampant. Because many of these students believed that they weren't smart and didn't have intelligence, because they believed they were stupid and not good enough, school for them was a painful experience. What they were experiencing in school often reinforced these beliefs. After all, if you are taking four courses and failing in three, it's easy to conclude that you're not smart enough and don't have intelligence.

As these seniors walked into the library where our 6½ hour session would be held, their shoulders slumped, they made very little eye contact and when they sat down their body language screamed, "I don't want to be here. This is a waste of time." In fact, six students went to Peg to see if they could get out of the session.

I welcomed them and introduced that during our time together they would discover power within them to make a positive difference in their lives, school experience and relationships. They didn't seem to be convinced. The message I was getting from them was, "I'm here, but I'm not participating." But this was before they met Jenny Severson, my training partner and a facilitator for Quantum Learning. They didn't know that Jenny's genuine respect for students and positive strategies for engaging students would result in their remembering who they are at their core, discovering and developing their potential, and expressing the uniqueness of their spirit-to-be.

As Jenny guided them through several activities, they became aware of their incredible ability to learn. They learned how to activate their brain, how to stay engaged and how to interact in meaningful ways with others. Not only were they not sleeping, listening on their headsets, or playing with their phones, but focused and actively participating, taking risks by asking questions and sharing what they were learning, and, most wonderful of all, smiling and laughing.

Why are students coming to school? If we are only paying attention to the outer lives of students, if we are only noticing their appearance (slumping shoulders, no eye contact, homework not done, head on their desk), we can be misled and miss what they are really wanting from school. However, if we can look deeper into the inner lives of students, we will realize that **they are coming to school to know, discover, develop and express their unique spirit-to-be.** Students need teachers to promise that this will happen when they come to school. Top 20 teachers like Jenny keep that promise.

Students and teachers have something in common: handicaps. As teachers, we have handicaps that get in the way of our teaching. Our students have handicaps that get in the way of their learning. Sometimes their handicaps get in the way of our teaching and our handicaps get in the way of their learning.

> "If students are not learning, education is not happening....Though it is too often forgotten, the core business of schools is to improve the quality of students' learning."
>
> —Ken Robinson

Helen Keller and Anne Sullivan represent a student-teacher relationship where handicaps could have very easily prevented the discovery, development and expression of a student's unique spirit-to-be. Given that Helen couldn't see, couldn't hear and couldn't speak, her frustration in learning and Anne's frustration in dealing with such profound roadblocks could have prevented this teacher from unlocking the incredible potential of a gifted student.

The question is not: "What is wrong and how do we fix it?"
The question is: "What is possible and how do we create it?"

Fortunately for Helen and the senior class at a Native American school, they had teachers focused on the second question. Anne, Peg and Jenny's frustration in having to deal with their students' handicaps to learning was trumped by their belief in their students' ability to learn and express what is possible in their spirit-to-be. The power of their belief is the gift that they gave their students, a gift that empowered their students to discover what is possible and how to create it.

In Helen's case, we know that this discovery led to her using her 'handicaps' as a gift for unlocking the potential of similarly 'handicapped' people throughout the world. None of this would have happened without a teacher remembering who her student was at her core, discovering and developing her potential, and expressing the uniqueness of her spirit-to-be. This is the role of a teacher for 21st century students in American schools.

Where Are Students When They Come to School?

The question introducing this section is not intended to determine physical geography of students when they come to school, but the brain physiology of students. Only recently has modern technology enabled us to understand the human brain as never before. What is going on in this incredible world inside a student's head? Where are students in their brain regarding their experience of school?

We know that the human brain has two primary goals: survive and thrive. The survive mode of our brain looks for threats to physical and emotional survival. It operates in this fashion 24-7 without requiring any effort or conscious thought from its owner. A small part of our brain called the amygdala is in charge of this operation. It operates as a scout. It narrows its focus to look for signs of threat or danger while ignoring signs of opportunity. When the 'scout' perceives danger or threat, neurochemical activity occurs in the brain that results in the production of chemicals including adrenaline and cortisol. These chemicals ready a person to deal with the threat by fight or flight. Although cortisol helps us to survive, it also impairs cognitive ability.

On the contrary, the thrive mode of our brain looks for opportunities to grow, discover, explore, create, be in awe and appreciation. The thrive mode focuses on learning and reach-

> "Our primitive minds still perceive the world around us in terms of threats to our well-being or opportunities to find safety."
>
> —Simon Sinek

ing our full potential. When the thrive mode senses learning opportunities, neurochemical activity again takes place. This time dopamine takes center stage. Dopamine is the "happy" chemical that makes us feel good. The excitement that it causes results in our desire to engage in certain activities.

As important as each of these modes is, the survive mode is more important than the thrive mode. Unless we survive, thriving is of little value. Consequently, whenever threat is perceived and our survive mode activates adrenaline, our thrive mode becomes less active. Engaging in discovery, exploration or learning is no longer of interest. **Survive trumps thrive.**

So where are students in their brain when they come to school? Is their thrive mode actively squirting dopamine causing them to be excited and engaged in learning opportunities? Or has their survive mode sensed threat resulting in their inability to learn and causing them to disengage in school? While on her way to visit Grandmother, Little Red Riding Hood was in the thrive mode of her brain. However, upon entering Grandmother's cottage, she had 'a strange…uneasy' feeling. This young girl's survive mode got activated, and she began to sense a threat.

Numerous experiences outside of school activate our students' survive mode. These experiences make learning difficult for countless students. However, the purpose of this book is to focus solely on what students are experiencing in school that activates their survive mode and what we as teachers may be doing to cause this. To the extent that this is taking place, is there anything we can do to minimize its negative impact on them? Can we create such safety and trust in American schools that our students' thrive mode trumps their survive mode and learning becomes the norm for all students? The intention of this book is to pursue these questions in good company. My hope is that such a pursuit will move us closer to a 'yes' answer to this last question.

CHAPTER FOUR

Encountering My First Wolf in School

I met my first wolf in first grade. I never went to kindergarten. It wasn't offered in the four-room schoolhouse for grades one through eight I attended growing up in Dalzell, Illinois. On the first floor, grades one and two were in one room and grades three, four and five in another. Grades six, seven and eight were in the one classroom upstairs.

Only 12 of us started first grade in 1953. One of those was my friend Kenny. Our first grade teacher was also the principal who had been at the school for a long time. It didn't seem like she was ever happy. She always carried a thick ruler in her hand that she referred to as 'hard candy'. Whenever a student wasn't doing what she wanted, our teacher would give the student  some hard candy. She must have thought that Kenny had a sweet tooth. He frequently received our teacher's hard candy…sometimes across his knuckles, sometimes across his behind.

One fall morning in second grade, Kenny received several doses of hard candy. When we came in from recess, our teacher only counted eleven of us. "Where's Kenny?" she barked. I knew, but remained silent. My silence was of no help to my friend. Looking out the window, our teacher spotted Kenny running through the cornfield that bordered the school property. Unfortunately the corn had already been picked. Had it not, he could have managed his escape running through the tall rows of cornstalks. Kenny was an easy target. Two eighth grade boys were summoned by our teacher to track him down and return him to school. Kenny's freedom didn't last long.

Years later when I read Thoreau's essay on civil disobedience, I thought of Kenny. My young friend was my first hero. Unfortunately, my first hero was also my first experience of a school casualty. Kenny's spirit-to-be never made it through school. Some form of the wolf seemed to show up in his life during every day of school, including but not limited to his daily dose of hard candy.

Although I witnessed as a bystander the wolf going after Kenny in first and second grade, my first experience of the wolf coming after me was in fifth grade. I had been home from school for a few days with the flu. When I was feeling well enough to return to school, my parents insisted that I was not yet healthy enough to play in the basketball game that night. After informing my fifth grade teacher, who was also my coach, that I could be in school, but couldn't play in the game, he said, "Paul, you have a yellow streak down your back."

Although knowing that I wasn't afraid to play basketball, I felt confused and humiliated in front of my coach and teammates. What did my coach's comment mean?

"Oh, Grandmother, what strong judgments you make."

"Better to cause self doubt in you," said the wolf.

I was fortunate. My wolf experiences were minor compared to Kenny's and countless other students in American schools. Whereas Kenny encountered the big, bad wolf, I only encountered the whelp. Maybe that's why I almost always liked school and was engaged in learning.

My granddaughter Maggie hasn't experienced either the wolf or the whelp. She was in kindergarten last year. When she came to our home one day in June, I said to her, "Maggie, you look so sad. Did something happen?"

As a tear rolled down her cheek, she spoke through her grief, "Today is the last day of school."

I hugged her and smiled, hoping I would have the same experience with her after first grade and every grade thereafter. Chances are that the wolf will show up between now and then and her experience of sadness on the last day of school will only be a memory. But today Maggie's spirit-to-be is still alive and flourishing because a teacher didn't let the wolf get into her kindergarten classroom.

CHAPTER FIVE

More Than Anything Else, School Is...

For decades countless efforts have been made and billions of dollars have been spent to improve American schools. After a massive national effort like No Child Left Behind (NCLB), we continue to see minimal if any increases in student learning and achievement. Although certain improvements have been made by individual schools, as an educational system we seem to have made very little progress. That reality offers another unanswerable question: Why is that?

Ken Robinson suggests that an answer to this question may be that we have a septic focus, "the tendency to look at a problem in isolation from its context....The septic focus is clearly evident in the education reform movements like NCLB that focus on certain parts of the system while neglecting the system as a whole."[10]

A part of our septic focus may be that we do not yet understand what students are essentially experiencing when they attend American schools.

There are 15 schools within one mile of my home in St. Paul, Minnesota, and over 100 schools within ten miles. If you drive in my neighborhood between 7:30 and 8:30 a.m. Monday through Friday, you see kids going to school...walking to school, riding bikes to school, skate boarding to school, getting rides from parents to school, taking buses to school. For 180 days each year they spend approximately 1,080 hours in school buildings and on school grounds. During 13 years from kindergarten to senior year in high school, that's over 14,000 hours. Students spend about 13% of their life in school.

What happens during that time? What is really going on in American schools? More than anything else, what is school about? I have asked hundreds of students and adults those questions, and the answers vary from person to person. Here's a list that would be generated from a typical group of students and adults:

Learning	Boredom	Romance	Drama (not the class)
Testing	Preparation for future	Teaching	Skill development
Playing	Cheating	Socializing	Lunch
Studying	Caring	Bullying	
Listening		Sleeping	

All of these and more are things that go on every day in American schools. But more than anything else, what are American students experiencing between kindergarten and senior year in high school?

School is a social event in which students are compared and judged. School is a 14,000 hour public experience where students on a regular basis and in a variety of ways are either judging or comparing themselves or are being judged and compared by others. Almost everything about a student is compared or judged for 13 years. As such, it can be the most terrifying wolf that Red Riding Hood will ever experience in her life.

Here is a partial list of the many areas about which students are compared or judged:

Comparison of Academic Ability or Performance

Intelligence	Homework
Grades	Classes (AP, college prep, remedial, special ed, IB)
Test scores	Post high school plans (college, junior college, work, military)
Skills	Asking questions in class; needing help
Honor roll/National Honor Society	

Comparison of Athletic or Co-curricular Ability or Performance

Who made the team or got the lead in the play? Who is a starter or a substitute? Who is getting a scholarship? Who is captain or All-State?	What is the status of various activities (chess team or football; drama or hockey; quiz bowl or skateboarding; science fair or 4H; band, cheerleading or student council)?

Signing Day occurs when exceptional athletes are first able to announce the college or university they will be attending to play their sport. These announcements have become so important that ESPN shows up at high schools to do a live broadcast of the young athletes' decisions. The entire student body flows into the gymnasium to witness which college cap their beloved athletic hero will put on as he makes his decision public. Meanwhile, the students who organized the Thanksgiving food drive or the Christmas clothing drive sit in anonymity. Some things are more valued than others.

Comparison of Physical Appearance

Looks Weight Strength Size (tall or short) Complexion	Hair ("When my hair looks awful, I get stressed and sit there messing with my hair.") Tattoos/piercings Body parts

Social Comparisons

Friendships Dating Relationships with teachers Where they go for spring break or vacations	Who they sit with during lunch Weekend plans or activities Who gets invited and who doesn't Interests (music, sports, arts)

Other Comparisons

Family	Jobs
Parents	Hobbies
Siblings	Diet
Neighborhood where they live	Cell phones/I-pads/computer
House they live in	Clothes
Sexuality	Cars/bikes
Religion	Backpack
Race	Jewelry
Nationality	

Studies show that the number one fear that people have is the fear of public speaking. People are terrified of speaking to a crowd. The fear of public speaking rates higher for most people than the fear of death. Yet 'public speaking' by their performance or appearance is what students do every day in school. During these 'public speaking' moments, students are judged and compared. Almost everything a kid does in school is viewed and assessed by others. In a sense, when students enter school each day, they are given a microphone and expected to perform on stage. What goes on while students are in classrooms, lunchrooms or gymnasiums or while they are walking down the hall or standing in front of their lockers is a form of 'public speaking.' **Nothing happens more frequently in American schools than judgment and comparison.**

In her fabulous book, *Daring Greatly,* Brene' Brown claims, "What makes this constant assessing and comparing so self-defeating is that we are often comparing our lives…to unattainable, media-driven visions of perfection, or we're holding up our reality against our own fictional account of how great someone else has it."[11] When this occurs, our students develop a constant sense of being 'less than' which, over time, destroys their sense of worthiness.

Long before students enter high school, their status and worth have been established both by their own sense of themselves and by how others view them. More damaging than hard candy is the subtlety of the wolf's presence in judgment and comparison.

Not Good Enough

What is the net effect of this experience? More specifically, what happens to the inner life of a student when he experiences constant judgment and comparison for 13 years? Obviously that differs for each individual student. However, the most common conclusion that students seem to make from judgments and comparisons is that they are **not good enough.** Even the valedictorian, the all-state captain of the football team and the homecoming queen will conclude that they are not good enough.

> "We shape our institutions and then they shape us."
> —Winston Churchill

The experience of having to be on 'stage' and being judged in a public arena is the encounter of the wolf that creates the 'strange' and 'uneasy' feeling and eventually creates fear in students. Being in a place for six hours a day where they need to know something or know how to do something and knowing that they don't know something or don't know how to do something creates an uneasy feeling. **Not to be good enough is terrifying.**

Being not good enough is equivalent to being **not like** everyone else, or, in other words, abnormal. This sentiment provides a perfect stomping ground for the wolf. When the students are on stage, the wolf's teeth are sharp and visible because the students' feelings of not being good enough and of being abnormal are likely to be activated. **Being judged and compared are the threats students experience in American schools.**

What do students who find themselves in this situation do? What do students do when they believe and feel that they are not good enough, but continue to be in a place where they are compared and judged? The solution to the problem of fear and terror of not being good enough is to disappear or become invisible. In order to survive, students must disengage. **Disengagement is a strategy activated by the survive mode of our students' brains when they perceive threat.**

Our students' belief that they are not good enough is actually a form of shame. "When shame descends," asserts Brene' Brown, "we almost always are hijacked by the limbic system. In other words, the prefrontal cortex, where we do all of our thinking and analyzing and strategizing, give ways to that primitive fight-or-flight part of our brain."[12]

Strategies for Becoming Invisible

When the normal school experience for students is being publicly judged for their performance or appearance and they begin to feel like they are not good enough, they will identify and intentionally use strategies to become invisible. **Invisibility and disengagement become emotional and psychological survival strategies for countless students in American schools.** With this need to survive, learning is not only irrelevant but also impossible for numerous students.

Let's consider some specific examples of how students strategize to be invisible in school.

Blue Shirt Boy: Linda Levitt, a professor at Arizona State University, had the following experience with her middle school son. When the school year ended, she noticed that he was growing out of his clothes and that they would have to do some shopping before the next school year. Since he seemed to be growing so rapidly, they decided to wait until closer to the opening of school. A few weeks before school began, she offered to take him shopping. The boy asked his mother to wait until school began. She assumed he wanted to see what other students were wearing before buying new clothes.

When her son came home from the first day of school, he informed his mother that he was ready to go shopping, but that he only wanted to buy blue shirts. Upon asking him why only blue shirts, he said that the walls in his classrooms were blue.

This student was not interested in wearing what his peers were wearing, but wanted to wear something that would result in his not being noticed. He had an intentional strategy to be invisible. He didn't want the wolf to see him.

Photo Fear: Kevin enjoyed playing soccer as a youngster. His dad worked with him on his soccer skills and formally coached Kevin from a very young age. As he got older, Kevin's primary goal was to make the high school varsity team. In a school of 2,000 students, that was quite the challenge. Each year he played hard, but could feel the anxiety increase as tryouts drew near.

Many of Kevin's friends checked in on him during soccer tryouts. They wanted to know what team he made. During his junior year, he tried out, but did not make the varsity team. As a member of the junior varsity that year, his team picture was published in the school yearbook.

A year later, with both his hopes and anxiety levels high, Kevin tried out for the coveted varsity soccer team. Although he made it through a number of practices, in the end he was cut from the team. Through the defeat and in the face of many questions from friends, Kevin played his senior year on the junior varsity team.

When picture day came, the day where he would be immortalized in the school yearbook for **not** being on varsity, he found himself in the midst of a blatant, calculated lie. Kevin told his coach that he didn't have his jersey but, since he lived only a mile from school, he would go home to get it in time for the yearbook photo. As he had planned, Kevin left for his jersey and intentionally delayed his return to the field until the photographer was leaving and the team was gearing up for practice. He successfully missed the team photo that would later be found in the high school yearbook.

The fear that the wolf instilled in Kevin of not being good enough because he was on the junior varsity team as a senior resulted in his strategy to be invisible for the team picture. He thought that if he were in that team photo, he would forever be noted as not being good enough.

Trombone Terror: Dan Gerard tells the story of learning to play the trombone when he was nine years old.

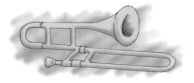

"I was volunteered to perform in a school play. It wasn't my idea and I didn't see any way around it. I practiced for a week straight and thought I was ready. On the day of the performance, I was so nervous I felt physically sick. I didn't want to do the performance. I wanted to die.

"So, I took a small hammer and dented the slide of the trombone enough so that it wouldn't slide. I showed up to school with my 'altered' instrument and proceeded to tell an elaborate story about how my trombone was damaged. Luckily there were no spares and I was allowed to skip my performance."

As an adult, Dan commented on his experience:

"While this is a legitimate fear, the reality is that you aren't the only one to feel this and it's OK to feel this way. The truth is, your audience does NOT want you to fail. They want you to succeed. And even if you do make a mistake, they will be understanding. The crowd will not mock your mistakes."

Although Dan's assessment is sometimes true, it is not always true. Imagine a basketball player taking a shot and not even hitting the rim. The opposing fans' response is likely to be: "Air ball...air ball...air ball." The wolf can show up as a mocking crowd.

We've asked thousands of people the following questions:

- Have you ever tried to become invisible in school?
- Why?
- What were your strategies?

Answers to these questions range from amusing to disturbing. A woman in St. Louis said that she sat behind the boy with the big head. When the teacher in the front of the room would walk in one direction, she would move her head in the other direction. The boy's big head shielded her from the wolf.

A recent college graduate said she hung out with a loud and funny group of friends. Being quiet herself, she felt that nobody would notice her among her boisterous friends.

My own strategy was to take notes. While Fr. Theodore was lecturing on the history of the Roman Empire, I would pretend to be furiously taking notes. I figured that he would think I was so interested in what he was saying that he wouldn't call on me and interrupt my note taking.

A more alarming strategy was shared by a woman who attended one of our training sessions and had laughed as others shared various humorous examples of strategies to be invisible. However, approaching me during a break, she said she didn't want to share her story publicly, but felt it was important that teachers realize that not all strategies to be invisible are lighthearted and innocent.

Her story took place during her sophomore year in high school. She noticed that her teacher never called on the students who were considered druggies. Wanting to avoid being called on in class, she decided to start dressing like the druggies. After a few weeks of looking like them, she began to draw some attention from the druggies. She would even be invited to sit with them during lunch. Being a shy girl without many friends, she willingly took them up on their offer. Before too long they invited her to their parties where she began to experiment with drugs. She felt a sense of belonging in this group and moved deeper into the drug culture for the rest of her high school and college years. She finished her story by saying: "One way to

distract yourself from the feeling of not being good enough is to drown it with booze and drugs."

More than anything else, school is a social event in which students are compared or judged. If that comparison or judgment results in students believing that they are not good enough, they will find ways to disappear and disengage. Unfortunately for many of our students, that's exactly what happens.

Not Smart Enough

One of the most frequent and possibly the most damaging threat the wolf provides for students has to do with their sense of their own intelligence.

Wayne Dyer, in his book *Wishes Fulfilled*, writes, "You very likely have a conceptual framework of just how smart you are and have carried that belief in you since you were a youngster in elementary school."[13] Although there are certainly exceptions to this, I believe this is true for most people. Both students and adults have a sense of their intelligence and that sense most likely was formed when they were in elementary school. Furthermore, it seems that what people perceive their intelligence to be is less than what their real intelligence actually is.

This limited yet powerful sense of our intelligence is likely determined by comparisons we make with others and the feedback we receive from teachers and other significant adults.

Our understanding of intelligence, claims Ken Robinson, "has become dangerously narrow and other intellectual abilities are either ignored or underestimated."[14] Nonetheless, because these standards have been in place for so long, they are seen as the absolute measure of intelligence.

"Children with strong academic abilities," continues Robinson, "often fail to discover their other abilities. Those of lower academic ability may have other powerful abilities that lie dormant. They can all pass through the whole of their education never knowing what their real abilities are. They can become disaffect, resentful of their 'failure' and conclude that they are simply not very bright."[15]

Because school is a place where intelligence matters, students who believe they are low on the totem pole need to become invisible in order to deal with the feeling of not being smart enough.

One high school senior had a strategy for accomplishing this: apathy. During a serious conversation with teachers about what he was experiencing in school, this boy said, "It's better to be numb than dumb." When he was asked to explain what he meant by this, he asserted that teachers determine who is dumb. Teachers determine what is right and wrong on tests; they determine the grade a student gets; they have the red pen. In order to maintain power in his life, he could choose to be numb, to be apathetic and to not (at least on the surface) care.

If he was told that if he didn't do his homework he would fail the class and have to attend summer school, his response would be, "I don't care."

We are often fooled by our students' apathy. We think they don't care. What we often don't realize is that apathy is a strategy to deal with matters they do care about. Apathy is a power that enables some students to handle the belief that they are not smart enough.

"What we know matters," writes Brene' Brown," but who we are matters more. Being rather than knowing requires showing up and letting ourselves be seen. It requires us to dare greatly, to be vulnerable."[16] However, when our students identify themselves as not good enough, they choose not to dare, are fearful of being vulnerable, decide not to show up and strategize ways to not be seen. Their courage to learn erodes and they disengage.

PART 2

THE INNER LIFE OF STUDENTS

CHAPTER SIX

The Influence of Messages and the Power of OPOs

Throughout history, courageous men and women have risked their lives for the sake of discovery. The desire to discover, explore and know is wired into the core of who we are as human beings. Although there is so much to be discovered, what is the most important discovery that our students can make?

The most important discovery that our students can make is to discover WHO THEY ARE.

The most important people in their life are those people who help them discover WHO THEY ARE.

The Power of the Social Mirror

During our life-long journey to discover the truth of who we are, we encounter numerous revelations and dangers. The dangers are put in our way by the wolf who is intent and set on us never discovering our true selves. The wolf knows that once we discover the truth of who we are, his power to govern us by fear is greatly diminished.

A primary and powerful strategy used by the wolf to prevent self-discovery comes from the Social Mirror and OPOs—Other People's Opinions.

Individuals discover the truth of who they are in numerous ways. These include family and relatives, friends and classmates, teachers and coaches, involvement in school and church, participation in extra-curricular activities and organizations, life experiences, the media, and so on. These are all part of our social mirror that reflect to us an image of who we are. The primary way these reflections appear is through messages. In other words, an important way we come to know who we are is by verbal and non-verbal messages stemming from the opinions of other people.

Let us think of our students and ourselves as message centers. Thousands of messages bombard us each day. Some messages are important; some are trivial. As in the Parable of the Eagle, the most important messages are those dealing with who others think we are or want us to be. Some of these messages are obvious; others are not.

As a message center we need to understand some very important things about messages. First, messages have power. Messages draw our attention. By doing so messages have influence regarding what we focus on. They influence what we think about and how we think. For example, an advertisement about a car focuses not only on a particular mode of transportation, but also on the status we will have or the pleasurable experience we will enjoy by owning this car.

The Validity and Interpretation of Messages

Another important consideration regarding messages is their validity. Is the message true or false? Each message that comes to us is also interpreted by us as being either true or false. The validity of the message and our interpretation of the message create four possibilities.

1. If you receive a **false** message but interpret it as **true**, you are now believing what is **false**.

2. If you receive a **true** message but interpret it as **false**, you are now believing what is **false**.

3. If you receive a **true** message and interpret it a **true**, you are now believing what is **true**.

4. If you receive a **false** message and interpret it as **false**, you are now believing what is **true**.

Because we are a message center, the quality of our lives and relationships is greatly influenced by how well we interpret the validity of messages. When we are operating as a Top 20 and thinking and learning more effectively, we are more adept at interpreting true messages as true and false messages as false. If we are able to do this, we will enhance the quality of our lives. If we are operating as a Bottom 80, we will more often interpret true messages as false and false messages as true. As such, we will diminish the quality of our lives and relationships.

Messages are powerful because they form us. They form the way we see ourselves. They form our opinions, attitudes, and beliefs. If all of these important things are being formed by what is false, they will have a negative impact on our lives. If they are being formed by what is true, they will have a positive impact on our lives.

Interpreting Messages

Recall the parable of the eagle in chapter 3. The messages sent to the eagle in this story have a powerful influence. More powerful than the messages, however, is the eagle's own interpretation of the validity of the messages. The eagle's interpretation of the messages it received became its beliefs.

1. If you receive a false message ("You are a chicken."), but interpret it as true ("I am a chicken."), you are now believing what is false ("I am a chicken.").

2. If you receive a true message ("You are an eagle.") and interpret it as false ("No, I'm not."), you are now believing what is false ("I am not an eagle.").

3. If you receive a true message ("You are an eagle.") and interpret it as true ("I am an eagle."), you are now believing what is true ("I am an eagle.").

4. If you receive a false message ("You are a chicken."), but interpret it as false ("No, I am not."), you are now believing what is true ("I am not a chicken.").

The eagle's full potential and the quality of its life are influenced by the messages it receives, but determined by the eagle's own beliefs about those messages. If the farmer sent the message that the eagle was a chicken but the eagle responded, "Wrong. You're mistaken. I'm an eagle," then the farmer's message would have no power over the eagle.

As it is for the eagle, the same is true for us. The messages we interpret as true become our beliefs and have a powerful influence on our life. True messages that become our beliefs will help us develop our potential. False messages that become our beliefs will block our potential.

Brene' Brown comments on the danger this can become for us: "We all have good and bad, dark and light, inside of us. But if we don't come to terms with our shame, our struggles, we start believing that there's something wrong with us—that we're bad, flawed, not good enough—and even worse, we start acting on those beliefs."[1]

Glen's False Belief

Glen was my driver taking me to a hotel in San Diego for a conference with teachers and principals. He was a friendly 57-year-old man who served in Viet Nam on an oil tanker. He had enlisted when he was 17-years-old.

Once he learned that I was an educator, he told me he was good with his hands, but not very smart. During our 45-minute ride, he shared a few stories about solving challenging mechanical problems during his duty on the oil tanker. After pulling up to my hotel, we got out and walked to the back of the car. As he opened the trunk for my bags, I said, "Glen, before I go I have to tell you something. You have intelligence." Seeing the wonder in his eyes, I knew he had never been told that before.

"You've given me examples," I continued, "when you solved problems with your hands. But before your hands solved those problems, the intelligence in your brain told your hands what to do. You have intelligence. I work with my hands too. I'm an author. I use my hands to type out books. But before my hands can do that, the intelligence in my brain has to tell my hands what to type."

Squinting his eyes in wonder, he asked, "Do you mean there are different levels of intelligence?"

"That's not quite what I'm saying," I replied. "Not different levels, but different kinds of intelligence. Glen, are you right or left handed?"

"I'm right handed," he said.

"Well, I'm left handed. I have a strength in my left hand and you have a strength in your right hand. So who is strong, you or me?"

"Seems like we both are," added Glen.

"Yes, just in different ways. The same thing is true about our intelligence. We're both smart, just in different ways."

"When you were in school, Glen, why did you think certain kids were smart?" I asked.

"That's easy," he said. "They were good at math, could read and knew lots of stuff that the teachers were talking about."

"These students are smart, Glen. They have a kind of intelligence, but not the only kind. I want to apologize to you, Glen. Sometimes teachers like me have failed to tell students like you that there are different kinds of intelligence. I'm sorry that didn't happen, but today I want you to know that you have intelligence."

"You're a brave man, too," I said as I reached to shake his hand and noticed tears welling in his eyes. "Thanks for the ride, Glen, and thanks for serving our country."

As I walked up the steps of the hotel to present to 500 educators, I wondered how many of our students had never been told that they have intelligence. How many believe that being good with their hands means that they are not smart? Numerous Glens are in all of our schools.

Ken Robinson sounds the alarm when he reminds us that: "Many highly intelligent people have passed through the whole of their education feeling they aren't and many academically able people who've been feted by the system have never discovered their other abilities. Almost all of them have no real sense of their true creative potential. The waste of creative talent is a growing calamity."[2]

Influence

Influence is a subtle, but awesome power that changes the action or thinking of another person. Sometimes the Influence is direct and intentional; sometimes it's indirect and unintentional. Sometimes someone's influence is in our best interest and sometimes it's not. The opinions of teachers, peers and parents have a powerful influence on our students. If these opinions help students discover the truth of who they are, they will enable our students to soar. If they form false beliefs in our students, they will have a negative impact on our students' health, relationships and potential.

Young people need to remain mindful of the influence of others' opinions on them. They can do this by asking questions such as the following:

- What do the opinions of others have me doing or saying?

- What do they have me thinking or feeling?

- Where do they have me going?

- What do they have me becoming?

Think back to being in a group in grade school or high school. See if you recall something that became a value of that group, something you needed to have, a way you needed to act or a commonly used phrase.

What you remember is probably the result of group influence. Although you may not have been aware of this influence at the time, it was present and active. Perhaps the other group members weren't even aware of their influence on you. Nonetheless, influence was taking place.

> "Your 'coolness' is judged very early by your friends, by the dolls or trucks you have, or even if you have 64 or 96 colors in your crayon box. Later, it becomes clothes or cell phones. It starts with the media, but it comes down to the people we see every day, our peers."
>
> —Kayla

Some influence will nudge us in one direction, and some will nudge us in another direction. Top 20s have a sharp awareness of influence on them and the direction in which that influence is pushing. They also know that they are not completely controlled by influence. They still are free and responsible for making their own decisions. Jose Molina is an example.

The Blue Bear

I met Jose Molina on a flight from San Diego to Minneapolis. Jose was born in Guatemala and educated in Mexico and the United States. He worked for Shell Oil and was flying back to his home in London before heading off to India. Jose is a bright, thoughtful, and creative young man. His passion is developing potential in others, keeping alive their curiosity and empowering them to become entrepreneurs.

As is typical when sitting next to passengers on airplanes, I asked Jose about experiences he had in school. I'm looking for times when people may have encountered the wolf. His stories reminded me of times when the wolf had better beware of Little Red Riding Hood.

Jose began school when he was four-years-old. His teacher gave him a bear to color. Jose colored the bear blue with purple hands and sunglasses. When his teacher asked him why he colored the bear blue, Jose said that was how he saw the bear.

"But bears are not blue," said his teacher.

"How do you know?" asked Jose.

"Bears are brown, white or black," she said.

"How do you know? Have you ever seen a bear?" questioned the four-year-old.

"I have seen pictures of bears," she responded.

"You are seeing a picture of my bear…and my bear is blue."

You can't imagine the delight I experienced listening to Jose telling me this story as if he were four-years-old. The power of this young boy's imagination convinced me that some bears are blue. A few weeks after meeting Jose, I discovered Lynn Schooler's book *The Blue Bear: A True Story of Friendship and Discovery in the Alaskan Wild*. Jose was right.

Jose's second story was equally amusing. While in elementary school, he took a math test. When the test was returned to him, every answer was marked wrong and his grade was an F. As the teacher went through the test with the class, Jose realized that he had the right answer for every question. Approaching his teacher, he asked why the answers were marked wrong.

"Yes, you have the right answers, but you didn't solve the problems the way I taught you," she said.

"I found another way to get the right answers," responded Jose.

"But that's not the way you are supposed to do it," she argued.

"If you go from school to your house, is there only one way?" he questioned.

Jose's teacher ended the conversation claiming that he was being rude.

When he shared this experience with his father, Mr. Molina said, "Son, you are never to do anything just because someone wants you to do it that way." Jose's father was sending a warning to all wolves: Beware of boys who believe in blue bears.

Whereas Bottom 80 students are overly influenced by others, Top 20s are able to filter messages. Able to distinguish between messages that are true and messages that are false, they are less likely to be influenced in ways that are contrary to their best interest and to their true selves.

We need to help our students activate the power within them to discern which messages are shining lights along the path to developing their potential and discovering their true selves and which will limit their potential and creativity.

Intentions and Beliefs

The messages we send to our students reflect our intentions and beliefs. It may be that our intentions and beliefs about our students' ability and motivation are more powerful than anything else in American classrooms.

In her book, *Quantum Teaching: Orchestrating Student Success*, Bobbi DePorter refers to the hidden power of intention and asks teachers to reflect on their last teaching experience: "How did your intention (positive or negative) come through? Did you believe and act as if students wanted to be their best—that they can succeed, want to succeed and will succeed? Did you see through the image students project, and tap into what you know waits inside—their best selves? Did you interact with students while maintaining a positive intention about who they are and what they can be, and watch them rise to your expectations? All of these are evidence of your intention. And they count for as much or more than anything you say."[3]

Renate Nummela Caine and Geoffrey Caine state it this way, "Teachers' beliefs in and about human potential and in the ability of all children to learn and achieve are critical."[4]

Low self-esteem is often the result for many low-achieving and learning-disabled students. Far too often, negative school experiences have undermined their self-confidence and natural love of learning. They adopt various mantras:

- "I have a learning disability. I can't learn."

- "I'm a bad speller and I hate math."

- "English is dumb, why even try?"

In their minds, they see school as difficult, the teacher as the enemy, and they feel doomed to failure.

Imagine being sent to be Helen Keller's teacher. You meet a young girl who is blind, deaf and cannot speak. What is your belief? It would be reasonable to believe that this child will never learn. It would also be this 'reasonable belief' that would become the biggest handicap to her learning.

Anne Sullivan was sent to be Helen's teacher. What might her belief have been? Helping Helen learn is going to be difficult but she can learn. She saw Helen as handicapped but not disabled. It was Anne's belief that moved through the darkness that Helen was experiencing and unlocked the incredible potential residing in this young girl. As this potential manifested itself in Helen, she enlightened others to see and develop the untapped potential in millions of handicapped but able people.

The wolf understands the potential that resides in each student and the power of messages and beliefs in developing that potential. His intention is to use that same power of messages and beliefs to prevent student potential from being discovered and developed. In order to accomplish this goal, the wolf's strategy is to send students messages that form two powerful potential limiting beliefs:

I'm not good enough.

I'm not smart enough.

Chapters 7 and 8 explore ways by which these messages are sent, how these beliefs are formed, and what we can do to counter the wolf's vile strategies.

CHAPTER SEVEN

I'm Not Good Enough

A major opportunity for the wolf to create fear and cause disengagement in students occurs when they make mistakes. Having considered the powerful impact of messages and their influence in forming potential-activating or potential-destroying beliefs, we will now examine how messages and beliefs impact the very important human experience of making mistakes.

Our Top 20 team has trained over a half million people throughout the United States. A topic we often cover is about making mistakes. We ask participants to identify what other people (parents, teachers, coaches, other adults, siblings or peers) said or did to them when they made a mistake? Typically their answers to this question are similar to the following list:

Responses to Mistakes

Laugh	Shame
Yell	Loss of trust
Humiliate	Isolate or ignore
Disappointed	Angry
Punish (spanked, grounded, loss of privileges)	Judge
	Give 'the look'
Tell others	"What's wrong with you!"
Criticize	"What were you thinking?"
Bring it up over and over again	Called names: loser, dummy, stupid

All of these responses are messages…verbal and nonverbal messages. If these are the messages human beings receive when they make a mistake, what would be the belief they would form about themselves?

I'm not good enough.

The human experience of making mistakes commonly results in human beings believing that they are 'not good enough.' If we wanted to diminish the potential of American students, all we have to do is convince them that they are not good enough. The wolf has been hanging out in American schools and families doing just that. In our culture, making mistakes often results in people believing they are not good enough.

Knowing what is in store for them when they make mistakes, our students are left with one option: Don't ever make a mistake. The only way to do that is to not try. In other words, disengage.

In a sense, all learning is about risk taking. Learning is going outside our comfort zone to a place we have not yet been. Think of a small child learning how to walk, a kid trying to ice skate, a kindergartner learning to read, a middle school student at his first dance, a high school freshman in a foreign language class, a college student in a physics lab, a med student performing her first operation or an old man writing a book about the inner life of students. Learning makes us vulnerable. If the conditions are not believed to be safe, then the choice to be vulnerable is less likely to happen and engagement in learning will not take place.

Let us go back to the question posed at the beginning of this chapter: What did other people (parents, teachers, coaches, other adults, siblings or peers) say or do when you made a mistake? This question is not asking for all the bad things people might have done when we made a mistake. Nonetheless, the list of responses on page 59 includes only negative responses. Only rarely do people offer positive responses like: "They said it's OK to make a mistake" or "They helped me when I made a mistake."

When questioned further about this, people often admit to having received positive responses to their mistakes. However, the negative responses seem to have more power and a longer lasting impact. Why is that? I think it's because when people make mistakes they are vulnerable. They are wide open. A negative response in that situation is like a punch to the gut. It bowls us over. This is especially true when the mistake occurs in public. In these situations the survive mode of our brain takes over and the thrive or learning mode of our brain shuts down. The possibility of being humiliated by a mistake has the same effect. Our energies go to covering up, protecting or defending our selves.

Is it safe to make mistakes in school? If not, we will never create a culture of learning and the wolf would have devoured our students.

The Popcorn Story

One night when I was seven years old, I wanted to make popcorn. While my parents were watching TV in the living room, I undertook my cooking adventure in the kitchen. In those days microwaves were not an option. I had to make popcorn the old fashioned way. I put oil in a pan and placed it on the hot burner. Once the oil was hot, I reached up to pour popcorn seeds into the pan. When the plastic bag containing the popcorn seeds touched the hot pan, a hole melted in the bag and popcorn seeds spilled all over the stove, counter and floor.

Upon hearing the commotion, my parents rushed into the kitchen and immediately asked, "Are you OK?"

"Yes," I answered. Although startled by what had just happened, I had not been burned.

"Are you sure?"

"Yes, I'm fine," I replied.

"Good," said my parents. "We'll help you clean up the mess."

For the next few minutes we cleaned up the popcorn that had spilled. Then, after making popcorn a second time, we watched TV together in the living room.

My popcorn mistake and the way my parents responded to it had a powerful mental and emotional imprint on me and resulted in learning four lessons.

1. **I'm more important than a mess.** Because my parents' immediate concern was for my wellbeing and not for the mess on the floor, I experienced my value and worth.

2. **Be there when people make a mistake.** One of our responsibilities in life is to help others when they experience difficulties. It's not our responsibility to clean it up for them, but to support them in making things better.

3. **A lesson is in the mistake.** The lesson in my example is that heat melts plastic. In every mistake we make, life intends to teach us a lesson.

4. **Mistakes are wonderful.** Because many wonderful things can be learned from mistakes and risk-taking, they are to be valued, not avoided.

I was never consciously aware of this experience until my first year of teaching at the high school I had attended as a student. I was working with a bright senior English class on their writing. I'd read their papers at night and they were less than impressive. The next day I tried to get them to be more creative. Nothing seemed to work.

While reading their papers a few days later, I asked myself this question: "What's the difference between my students and me?" I was just out of college so there was only a four or five year gap between us. However, when I asked that question, my popcorn experience came rushing into my consciousness. In that moment I understood that the difference between my students and me was that I was not afraid of making a mistake.

With that awareness I realized that **my purpose as a teacher was to help my students fail**. Even as I write this sentence today, it sounds really strange. Aren't we trying to help our students succeed? Of course we are. However, if they are so afraid of failing, they will not move outside their comfort zone and develop their full potential.

Yes, one of our primary responsibilities as teachers, whether we are parent teachers, classroom teachers or coach teachers, is to help our students fail. We need to create a culture in which failure is viewed as a major way by which human beings learn important life lessons. We need to instill in our students a willingness to try and fail so they can develop skills and discover and create things that would otherwise never be discovered or created.

Failure is a natural way by which children learn. I recall my granddaughter Ellie taking her first step. What happened? She fell down. That's called failure. She wasn't trying to fall. She was trying to walk across the room. Then what? She got up and tried again. But, oops, down she went again. Failure. In her continued effort to walk and in her repeated failures, her legs got stronger and she gradually learned balance. Over time her failure led to success. No more falling. Had she feared failing, she would be a crawler her entire life.

Thomas Edison and the Wright Brothers were great at failing. Edison said: "I have not failed. I have just found 10,000 ways that won't work." Each of those 'ways that won't work' provided Edison with increased knowledge about what might work. Each failure was an opportunity to learn.

The Wright brothers had a similar experience. Even their planned first flight had to be delayed for weeks due to broken propeller shafts during engine tests. Wilbur's first attempt on December 14, 1903, stalled after takeoff causing minor damage to the plane. Following repairs, Orville, three days later, in what is considered to be the first flight, kept the plane in the air for 12 seconds. Then the plane 'fell down'. Yes, just like Ellie learning to walk, Orville and Wilbur tried again and again.

News Flash: I recently flew from Minneapolis to San Diego…a three hour flight…no crash!! "Orville and Wilbur, THANKS!! Your failures led to my success."

As a nation, a news flash such as this should be in newspapers and on news channels every day. We ought to have a national holiday called

Failure Day. Why? Because our nation has developed because men and women were willing to take risks, fail, make mistakes and learn how to do some incredible things.

Although renowned chemist Harry Kroto claims that 95 percent of his experiments fail, he doesn't believe that failure is the right word. Rather, he says, "You're just finding out what doesn't work."[5]

Unfortunately, we seem to have gone in the other direction. At home, in school and in the media, the messages that our young people get over and over again are that failure is to be avoided at all costs.

If you fail, you are a failure!
If you lose, you are a loser!

Imagine the Wright brothers hanging out with their friends on the evening of December 16, 1903, the night before their first flight, and informing them of their plans for the next day: "Hey, guys, come on over to Kitty Hawk tomorrow and watch us fly in an airplane."

Imagine their friends' sarcastic chuckles and comments: "Orville and Wilbur, birds fly. You guys are crazy. Human beings walk or ride horses. You're going to kill yourselves trying that foolishness. You'll go down in history as the Wrong brothers."

"Anyone who has never made a mistake has never tried anything new."

—Albert Einstein

Had the Wright brothers been governed by the opinions or beliefs of other people, they would have scrapped their ridiculous plan and, instead, tried making a more comfortable saddle. If such a scenario had taken place then, it would take us days to travel cross-country now.

If we are going to have future inventions in America, we need to have three teachers in every classroom: a caring adult, mistakes and failure. If any of these teachers are missing, our schools will not be cultures of learning.

But even more important than discovering, creating or inventing, we need to celebrate mistakes and failure so our students never form the belief that their mistakes and failures mean that they are not good enough, that they are inadequate or that they are stupid and don't have intelligence. We need to protect our students from the wolf who frequently shows up when mistakes are made or failure occurs. If we do this, then our students will be in the thrive mode of their brain, experience more dopamine squirts and enjoy life and learning more fully.

Awareness Leads to Change

Rachel Stafford shares a powerful and beautiful parenting story about transitioning the wolf within her to a woodsman. She relates how the wolf that resided within her would manifest itself in ways that scared her daughter and damaged her little girl's spirit-to-be. Although this is a story about a mother and daughter, it applies equally to our own relationship with students.

Being a perfectionist, Rachel came to believe that she was never good enough: "Holding myself to such unattainable standards weighed heavily on my soul and my inner turmoil eventually spilled out at people I loved the most." She expressed disappointment whenever her daughter made a mess. "My daughter was not allowed to be a child who learned by trying and…failing." Rachel justified her harsh responses to her daughter by believing she was helping her become responsible and preparing her for life.

Once when her children were playing in the basement, she heard her younger daughter crying hysterically. Running downstairs, Rachel angrily said to her older daughter, "What did you do?"

"My child didn't bother to explain that her little sister had slipped on the library book that was sitting on the bottom step. There really was no point. My beautiful child with humongous brown eyes that once held so much optimism looked defeated. Silent tears of a broken spirit slid down her face. My daughter knew it didn't matter what she said, she'd still be wrong; it would still be her fault."

Later, Rachel found her daughter crumpled up on her bed "like a dejected rag doll." Sitting on the edge of the bed, she said to her daughter: "I'm sorry…I feel mad inside a lot. I often speak badly about myself in my head. I bully myself….then I treat others badly—especially you. It is not right, and I am going to stop."

Rachel's strategy to change was one simple word: STOP. Whenever she would have a critical thought, "You look fat. You can't go out looking like that," she would be assertive to herself: "STOP. Only love today. Only love today."

After practicing this for a few days, Rachel's thinking became more positive and she let go of the need to control and criticize. She noticed her daughter beginning to try new things.

> She made doll furniture and clothing to sell in the neighborhood. She began baking new recipes without any help. Nothing she did was perfect. Nor was it mess-free or mistake-free, but the moment I said something positive, I saw her blossom a little more. That is when I began to clearly see beyond the mistakes and messes…noticing my child's inner beauty rather than looking for perfection on the outside….I began letting her be who she was meant to be instead of some idealistic version I had in my head….It's hard to become the person you're supposed to be when you aren't allowed to fall down and get back up.[6]

Because Rachel 'woke up', she not only realized the negative impact she was having on her daughter, but also realized that she had a choice. Although Rachel had been responding as a Bottom 80, she also possessed the power to respond as a Top 20.

Recall the Responses to Mistakes listed on page 59. Not only is it likely that people who receive these messages when they make a mistake will form the belief that they are not good enough, but it is also more likely that they respond to their own mistakes in Bottom 80 ways. Let's consider what those responses might look like.

Bottom 80 and Top 20 Responses to Mistakes

The wolf makes himself present in the responses to mistakes previously listed. Because these messages often communicate "you're not good enough," students are likely to practice four survival strategies.

They **deny** a mistake by verbally or mentally stating that it didn't happen or by hiding the evidence that it did. They don't talk about it. They block it out of their minds. If someone else brings it up, they deny it or get defensive.

When our students deny a mistake, it is because they do not want to be the recipients of the negative responses to mistakes. Using denial as a survival strategy is not a good decision, but it is certainly understandable.

They acknowledge the mistake, but **blame** someone else for it. This may take the form of "He did it" or "She made me do it." They blame in order to get off the hook. In blaming they avoid responsibility. This is another survival strategy to avoid the negative responses from others

When it's obvious that they made the mistake, they can't use the strategies of denial or blame. Therefore, their survival strategy is to **justify** the mistake by offering 'good' reasons or excuses for doing it. A student might justify a mistake by saying to a teacher, "I couldn't get my homework done last night because my family was celebrating my grandmother's birthday."

They **dwell** on a mistake by focusing on nothing else but the mistake. They allow the mistake to overwhelm them by playing it over and over again in their heads. They let the mistake define them: "I'm so stupid. I never do anything right. I'll never be able to get over this."

When our students are operating like Bottom 80s and responding to mistakes by denying, blaming, justifying or dwelling, they are unlikely to get the important life lesson that is available in the mistake. Consequently, they are more likely to repeat the mistake again and again. Life will offer them many opportunities to learn the lessons. With each subsequent mistake, however, the consequences tend to become more severe.

The challenge with Bottom 80 responses is that they make complete sense. Thinking back to the list of how others respond to our mistakes, who wouldn't want to avoid that turmoil? When we operate out of fear and ineffective-Bottom 80 thinking, we don't have the clarity of insight to see that we are unable to grow from the experience because we have not learned the lesson from the mistake.

Our students have another choice. They can operate like a Top 20, own the mistake and learn the lesson life is trying to teach them. They can use the mistake as a teacher: "I just made a mistake. What I can learn from this is that heat melts plastic." As such, they are not likely to repeat the mistake. Once the lesson is learned, there is no further need to focus on the mistake.

Barry Johnson is a seventh grade football coach at Buffalo Middle School. He had attended a Top 20 coaches' session that included this lesson on responding to students' mistakes. Following his team's first game, he sent us the following email:

> The lesson I learned about learning from mistakes has really affected me as a coach. Before our first 7th grade football game of the season, I gave a big pep talk about mistakes: "Guys, I can guarantee this: every one of us is going to make a mistake today. It's okay. It's how we learn. Let's not get down on each other when that happens. We're going to stick together."

> We sent our captains out to the middle of the field for the coin toss, and they returned telling us we were kicking off. During our first defensive series, our cornerback gets beat deep on 3rd and 9. I heard kids on the sideline say to the cornerback, "That's okay. That's how we learn."

> At halftime our captains go back to the middle of the field to meet with the officials about which team gets the ball to start

the second half. They come back to report that we are kicking off again. "WHAT?!" I asked the ref. He said our kids won the toss in the first half and elected to 'Kick' instead of 'Defer to the second half.' So the other team elected to take the ball of course in the second half when it was their turn.

Obviously as coaches we had blown it. This Top 20 lesson helped me immediately take the heat off our captains and their teammates didn't get upset. It's making me a better coach. It's making us a healthier, happier, more 'together' team. My kids are not afraid to make mistakes.

I told the kids I wanted them to go all out…make mistakes and learn from them. The kids really bought in. They really came together quickly I think because of it. And do you know what? We didn't have any off-sides penalties the whole game!

It's not like they make more mistakes because you say it's okay. They actually play with more confidence and maybe that even REDUCES the number of mistakes. I think players will play harder and try harder for teammates and coaches who they think care about them than they will for a coach who is intimidating and teammates who are critical.

Barry's players are not quitting; they are not disengaging. Barry has found a way to silence the survive mode of his players' brains and activate the thrive mode. The wolf never gets into their huddle. They play better because they are not afraid of making mistakes.

Isn't that what we want for our students? Don't we want them to keep trying? As long as they keep trying, they will get better…whether that's as a football team or as students. That's the difference that a Top 20 coach or a Top 20 teacher can make.

Comfort Zone

Why is how students experience mistakes so important? It has every-thing to do with Comfort Zone. All students need a Comfort Zone, a place where they are safe and where they know how to do what they need to do. On one hand our schools need to be Comfort Zones for kids. However, because it's easy for students to do things that are inside their Comfort Zone, they may not want to try things that are outside their Comfort Zone. Outside Comfort Zone is not only where students are more likely to make mistakes, but also where the Big Learning occurs. In order to get to the Big Learning, they need to pass through the land of mistakes.

If they experience negative responses whenever they make a mistake, they will stay locked inside their Comfort Zone.

When a second grade teacher asked her class a question, every student's hand went up. After the girl the teacher called on answered, her class-mates laughed. When it was time for school the next morning, the child informed her parents that she had a tummy ache. She actually had a heart ache. Because she had experienced the wolf in her classroom, she never raised her hand again.

Grace Murray Hopper said, "A ship in port is safe but that's not what ships are built for." Yes, our schools and classrooms need to be safe ports and Comfort Zones, but they also need to be wide-open oceans where students can explore and discover all sorts of wonderful and amazing things. However, if they are afraid of making mistakes, they are going to hang out in the safety of their Comfort Zone.

Sheryl was a pretty good basketball player in middle school, a speedy right-handed dribbler who could often get past her defender to the basket. Her coach frequently encouraged Sheryl to practice dribbling left-handed. Because she was uncomfortable dribbling left-handed and made more mistakes doing so, she refused to practice that way. Once she got to high school, her opponents realized she couldn't drib-ble left-handed. When they stopped her from dribbling to her right,

Sheryl's success on the court diminished considerably.

Taking risks and making mistakes is a Top 20 habit. The more students experience this, the more they learn and the easier it becomes. Learning from mistakes enables our students to succeed at higher levels. More importantly, it prevents them from getting stuck in a belief that they are not good enough.

Fear of OPOs and Failure

Unfortunately, not enough young people are meeting coaches or teachers like Barry Johnson. Rather, during their experiences of making mistakes, they meet the wolf, feel fear that keeps them locked in their Comfort Zone, and disengage. This debilitating fear often comes from two sources: OPOs (Other People's Opinions) and failure.

Tony is an all-too-common example of how OPOs govern a student's life. After hearing during morning announcements that tryouts for the chess team would be held after school, Tony shared with his friends at lunch that he was thinking about going out for chess. One of his buddies responded, "Thatta boy, Tony. You might want to get some pads to put on your elbows so you won't get bruised during your chess matches. I hear they'll give you a rook that you can sew on your letter jacket." Tony, being governed by his friend's OPOs, never showed up for the chess team tryouts.

What students like Tony need to know is: **Other people's opinions of me are none of my business unless they are in my best interest.**

Consider the frequency with which our students have been fully inhibited or even slightly affected through the wolf's presence in OPOs. Imagine how much potential has gone untapped and unfulfilled in American students.

Opinions are judgments about something that are not necessarily based on facts or knowledge. Our students should listen to the opinions of others but then discern if those opinions are in their Best Interest. If the opinions are in their Best Interest, they should act accordingly. If not, they should discount the opinions and make decisions based on their own desires or goals. Otherwise, they are allowing their lives to be governed merely by a thought that exists in someone else's head.

The fear of failure also keeps students stuck in their Comfort Zone, unwilling to try and often disengaged. The message in our culture is that failure is the worst thing that a person can do. This results in students believing, "If I fail, I am a loser." To help overcome this, the script we want students to internalize is:

Failure is an event, not a person.

Failure is something we do, but it is not who we are. However, the mindset of so many students is the exact opposite. Our culture highlights failures through mockery. When failures are mocked in the many cultural spotlights, it ignites the wolf and increases our students' fear to a point where failure is no longer an option. Unless we can convince our students of the truth that failure is something we do, but it is not who we are, we will never create a culture of learning.

The wolf's major strategy is to convince students that any form of failing means that they are a failure and a loser. Sharing with students examples such as Edison and the Wright brothers can demonstrate how failure can lead to discovery and achievement.

Abraham Lincoln is an example of this. Born into poverty, Lincoln was faced with defeat throughout his life. He lost eight elections, twice failed in business and suffered a nervous breakdown but became one of America's greatest presidents. Lincoln's road to the White House was anything but smooth.[7]

Although our students' own failures or losses may not have been as dramatic as Lincoln's, we need to help them identify failures in their lives (like falling down when learning to walk) that have lead to discovery, growth or an important lesson.

A.C.T.

How should we as adults (teachers, coaches, parents) act regarding mistakes others make or we make? The letters A, C and T suggest three things we should do to keep the wolf out of our schools, classrooms and homes.

A— Aware of Beliefs: The A stands for Awareness of our belief about our self as a mistake maker. What is this belief? It is important to know this belief because it will get activated when we or someone else makes a mistake. Awareness of this belief might help us make a better choice when it gets activated.

C— Conscious Choice: C stands for two Conscious Choices. The first is what 'conscious choice' will we make when **we** make a mistake? If we don't make a conscious choice, we are likely to make an unconscious choice: deny, blame, justify, dwell.

In order to make a conscious choice, it's helpful to know what our mental script is when we make a mistake. What are we likely to think or say when we make a mistake?

- "How can I hide this from my spouse?"
- "How can I blame this on someone else?"
- "How can I justify this to my boss?"

When Willow would make a mistake as a youngster, someone would say, "Willow, what's wrong with you?" Because children often take things literally, when she made a mistake she believed something was wrong with her. As she got older, whenever she made a mistake, she would say to herself, "Willow, what's wrong with you?"

Once she became aware of how dangerous and dysfunctional this was, she changed her script: "Oops. Look what I just did. Wonder what I can learn from this?" 'Oops' means that a mistake has been made. 'Look what I just did' means that I did it. 'Wonder what I can learn from this' is activating our curiosity to get the lesson.

Bottom 80 Script	Top 20 Script
"What's wrong with you?!"	"Oops! Look what I just did. I wonder what I can learn.

Our scripts are set, but they are not set in stone. It's great if we have a healthy, Top 20 script. It means we will more likely learn from mistakes and develop our potential. However, if we have developed a Bottom 80 script as Willow had done, we can consciously change it.

The second 'conscious choice' is what do we want to say or do when **someone else** makes a mistake, especially a child. If we don't make a conscious choice, we are likely to make an unconscious choice like those on the Responses to Mistakes list. Again, knowing our mental script is important. What are we likely to think or say when someone else makes a mistake?

Willow's Bottom 80 script, "What's wrong with you?" was activated when others made a mistake. When her son would make a mistake, she would say, "What's wrong with you?" Becoming aware of the harm this would cause in her son, she changed her script: "Hmm, what can we learn from this?" She wanted him to value mistakes and see them as opportunities for learning important lessons.

Jacki Streveler, a school counselor in Wausau, Wisconsin, shared how changing her script resulted in a healthier response to her daughter. After attending a Top 20 Training session, Jacki sent us this email:

> Our six-year-old missed the bus yesterday and instead of making her feel 'dumb and stupid', we made a conscious effort to let her know we were not mad at her and that we would help her discover what she can do differently next time. Today she was even making sure her older sister was listening to Mom's requests to get hats, coats, and mittens on in time for the bus. With both my husband and I reinforcing

the lesson and not the hurtful message of "what were you thinking," we had a happier, more confident six-year-old this morning who made the bus on time! Without your insight we might have been battling this for months and reinforcing negative thoughts in our little girl.

As was stated at the beginning of this chapter, during our presentations on mistakes, we ask adults to go back in time to when they were school age and identify how other people responded to them when they made a mistake. At one session for adults, a 14-year-old girl happened to be in attendance. After the group listed several negative responses to mistakes, we asked participants, "What happens to a person when he or she gets these negative responses?" The 14-year-old student quickly answered, "It's the end of innocence."

This is a very profound statement. Children go through life wide open, but when they experience negative responses, they begin to close themselves. This is why we need to realize that there are no neutral responses to a mistake. Every response to a mistake matters. If it's a Popcorn response like I experienced with my parents, it will keep a child open and engaged. If it's a humiliating response, the child will close up and disengage. Because there is no neutral response to a mistake, our responses need to be conscious and intentional.

T— Talk about It: 'T' stands for talk about it. When we make a mistake, can we talk about it with our family or students? "Class, you didn't do well on this test. I made a mistake in teaching this lesson. I'd like to talk about this and have you help me learn how I can do this better next time." Not only might we learn how to better teach the lesson, but we have just freed our students from the fear of making mistakes and set up an opportunity for the next time they make a mistake: "Hey, class, let's talk about the mistakes you made and see what we can learn from them."

While I was Director of Guidance and Counseling at St. Thomas Academy, our headmaster was John Greving, a leader who modeled talking about his own mistakes. John would sometimes come into administrative team meetings and say, "I just made a mistake. I want to talk about it and have you help me learn everything I can from this mistake."

Have you ever had a boss who said something like that? What a difference it made. It allowed me to go to the Headmaster at times and say, "I just made a mistake. I want to talk about it and have you help me learn everything I can."

Mistakes have been given a bad reputation. If we want to create a learning culture, we have to do everything we can to change this reputation. One way to do that is to talk about our own mistakes to our students and colleagues. By doing so, we take mistakes from under the rug and place them on a pedestal where they become common every day means by which we learn, grow and develop our potential.

Our students need administrators like John Greving, coaches like Barry Johnson, teachers like Jacki Streveler and parents like Rachel Stafford. With Top 20 adults like these in their lives, the wolf will be kept at bay. Our students will realize that making mistakes does not mean that they are not good enough but that they have an opportunity to take healthy risks, move outside their Comfort Zone and develop their potential.

CHAPTER EIGHT

I'm Not Smart Enough

I once met an incredibly intelligent woman. She was an outstanding communicator, a leader in her profession, an excellent reader and gifted writer filled with insights, savvy about technology, a skilled carpenter, an accomplished athlete and musician with a high level of social-emotional intelligence. However, due to the sense of her own intelligence, which she had formed in elementary school, she chose to be a physical education major in college instead of a history teacher. Her rationale for choosing this major was her belief that it was the only thing in college she would be able to handle. She didn't believe she was smart enough to be a classroom teacher. In her mind, by majoring in physical education her lack of intelligence would be easily hidden.* She had met the wolf and had come to believe in his lie.

The wolf's primary strategy to get students to disengage is to cause them to believe or feel that they are not good enough or smart enough. When students experience the mental or emotional pain or stress of not being good enough or smart enough, they will find strategies for dealing with those feelings. It's as if someone touches a hot burner on a stove and immediately pulls away.

A major way that students experience not good enough or not smart enough in school is by believing or feeling that they are stupid. Once this occurs, they will immediately begin to withdraw and disengage.

(* We believe that majoring in physical education is a challenging and complex subject matter that requires serious thought and rigor on the part of those engaged in this major.)

The big question we are trying to answer in this book is, "How do we engage disengaged students?" The best way is to keep them from disengaging in the first place. We can achieve this goal by keeping stupid in the box and not  having them ever believe or feel that they are not good enough or smart enough. This is a 'game changer' and will make a major difference in how students experience school. Students who feel stupid disengage. Students who don't feel stupid engage.

This chapter focuses on four questions:

1. What does stupid mean?

2. What do students do when they feel or believe they are stupid or not smart enough?

3. What causes students to feel or believe they are stupid?

4. What can we do about that? How can we keep stupid in the box or get it back in once it has gotten out?

What does stupid mean?

Students use the word 'stupid' in different situations.

They use it in academic or intellectual matters:
"I feel stupid when I can't multiply fractions."
"My grades are in the lowest quarter of my class. I must be stupid."

They use it in regards to physical or athletic situations:
"I feel stupid because I'm too tall…too short."
"I felt stupid when I dropped the ball."

Although students use the word 'stupid' in various situations, it almost always means the same thing: "I'm not good enough" or "I'm inadequate." We will never hear a third grader say, "I'm inadequate as a speller." Rather, he'll say, "I'm stupid at spelling."

What do students do when they believe or feel that they are stupid?

Students don't just believe or feel that they are stupid; they react to stupid. The reactions that are presented below have come from students themselves. We have asked hundreds of students what they do when they feel stupid (reactions or responses) and what they experience that results in them felling stupid (causes).

Student reactions to believing or feeling that they are stupid fall into eight categories.

1. **Quit:** The most common response students make to feeling stupid is that they quit. Some quit and leave (dropout) while others quit and stay (keep coming to school but do so without engaging). A study by Robert Balfanz and Vaughan Byrnes at Johns Hopkins University's School of Education estimated that 10 to 15 percent of American students (between 5 and 7.5 million) are chronically absent from school Chronic absence means missing 10% of the school year.[8] In Georgia, the District of Columbia, Mississippi, Nevada, New Mexico, and South Carolina less than two-thirds of students graduate from high school. New York City has 36,000 dropouts per year. Although feeling stupid is not the only factor influencing chronic absences or the drop out rate, it is a cause for many students.

Quitting doesn't only mean dropping out or being absent from school. Many students attend school on a regular basis but still find ways to withdraw or be invisible. I once met a student in a Boston middle school who was walking out of school at the end of the day on a Friday afternoon. I asked him what he had learned in school that day. He paused and said, "That's going to be a hard question to answer." After a few moments of silence, I thought I would bail him out, "Is there anything you learned this week?" He quickly responded, "Not really." He had been in school every day but was just going through the motions…one of the countless students who quit and stay.

2. **Pretend:** Students have figured out how to appear to be engaged without really being engaged. They are able to maintain eye contact with the teacher while mentally being on a beach. They can appear to be engaged by taking notes when they are actually writing a note to a friend. When asked by the teacher if they understand what is being taught, they can nod their head 'yes' although they are clueless about the lesson.

Adults are also prime candidates for pretending when they feel stupid. Have you ever not gotten a joke, but laughed anyway?

3. **Be emotional:** Students react emotionally to being stupid. They feel embarrassed, angry, upset, sad, worried, nervous or stressed.

4. **Make judgments:** Students make judgments about themselves. "I'm not good enough; I don't know anything; I'm bad at everything; I am stupid."

5. **Be defensive:** Students protect themselves by judging the class ("This class is stupid."), the teacher ("What a dork this teacher is.") or other students ("She's such a teacher's pet.").

6. **Attack:** Students argue with or challenge the teacher; they bully other students.

7. **Be motivated:** When students feel stupid, they are sometimes motivated to do better on the next test or assignment. However, they are still carrying stupid inside. We don't want students to study or be engaged because they feel stupid but because they are curious and want to learn.

8. **Be numb:** Because school is a place where intelligence matters, students who are at the bottom of their class rank need to become invisible in order to deal with the feeling of not being smart enough.

> "We numb the pain that comes from feeling inadequate and 'less than.'"
>
> —Brene' Brown

Earlier we gave an example of the high school boy who used apathy to accomplish this. For this student, as dysfunctional as it ultimately may have been, apathy allowed him to maintain a sense of power over his own life. In addition to apathy, students also choose drugs and alcohol for their numbing agents.

When we ask teachers if they have ever seen any of these eight symptoms in their students, they readily acknowledge the prevalence by which they appear. If we are constantly noticing the symptoms, then our students' feelings and beliefs that they are stupid or not smart enough has become an epidemic. American schools have become a breeding place for wolves.

What causes students to feel or believe that they are stupid?

Let's start with the most important statement I will make in this chapter: **stupid doesn't exist**. Every child, every student and every adult has intelligence. If that is true, then why do so many students and adults believe or feel that they are stupid? I'll answer that question with a very personal example.

I am often handed something to read. A friend or someone at a training might give me an article or a book and say, "Read page 17." Every time this happens, I have the same experience. I begin to read, get about a third of the way down the page, and then begin to feel stupid. I have thoughts like, "She thinks I should be done with this by now. I'm a slow reader. I feel stupid."

I read at a certain rate. Whatever that rate is, it is. I read slower than some people read and faster than others. My reading rate has nothing to do with being stupid. In fact, I consider myself a very good reader. I am able to comprehend what I read at a high level.

Why, then, do I feel stupid whenever someone asks me to read something? Try to imagine a place in my brain where my beliefs reside. Picture that place as a box. In that box is an Equal Sign. The Equal Sign means **I AM.** At times in my life when I have certain experiences, I go into this box, pull out the Equal Sign, and put it between whatever I am doing and stupid. It would look like this:

SLOW READING RATE = STUPID

In my mind it sounds like this: "Because I am a slow reader, I am stupid."

Even though stupid doesn't really exist, I can deem or equate myself to being stupid in certain situations. Another time I frequently have this experience is when I am dealing with anything mechanical like the engine of my car. Whenever I hear that strange sound coming from my car engine, I lift up the hood, scratch my head and immediately go to that box and pull out the Equal Sign.

In my mind it sounds like this: "I have no idea why the engine is making this noise or what to do about it. I'm so stupid." I immediately slam the hood down and call my automobile mechanic.

ENGINE NOISE = STUPID

If stupid doesn't exist, what does exist? Real experiences exist like reading at a certain rate and a car engine making strange noises. These have nothing to do with being stupid. However, when we have these experiences and pull out the Equal Sign, we attach stupid to these real experiences. If we didn't apply the Equal Sign, we would simply have experiences that would have nothing to do with being stupid.

So the real cause of stupid is pulling out the Equal Sign. If we didn't do this, stupid would stay in the box.

When asked when they felt stupid or situations that caused them to feel stupid, students offered hundreds of different responses. All of their answers could be put into one of five categories:

1. **Called**

2. **Comparison**

3. **Confused**

4. **Can't**

5. **Certain Situations**

These are times when the wolf appears in full force. Let's drill deeper into these five categories that cause students to believe or feel that they are stupid. We will consider examples that students gave for each category and how we might counter each cause in order to minimize the wolf's influence and the negative impact stupid has on our students.

1. Called

A major strategy used by the wolf to disengage students is to have students called 'stupid'. A student in our research said, "I feel stupid when I say something and others say it's stupid or someone says something and I don't know what they mean and they call me stupid."

In the world of students, 'stupid' has a number of synonyms. Teachers from different parts of the country have shared with us offensive words that students use in their schools that mean 'stupid'.

Dumb	Retard	Duh	Short bus
Idiot	Dork	Ignorant	Loser
Gay	Lame	Slow	Imbecile

These words are probably more dangerous than profanity, and we need to do whatever we can to keep them out of school. Unfortunately, some students are even called these things at home. A student said, "Every night my dad tells me I'm stupid. I wish I could leave."

Maybe one of the most damaging experiences students can have occurs when their answer to a question is followed by laughter. Uninvited laughter is a powerful response to students that can scar them for a lifetime and keep them from participating in class.

The damage that laughter or being called these words does to our students is incomprehensible. Nonetheless, many of our students frequently hear these words directed towards them. However, it's not only words that are being used to call students stupid. It would be rare to hear a teacher calling a student one of these words but she may knowingly or unknowingly communicate stupid nonverbally. Some teachers have perfected 'the look' or other expressions or gestures that result in students feeling stupid. Some of these include:

- Shaking our head
- Talking very slowly or very loudly
- Raising our eyebrows

Students also identify themselves as stupid based on grades they get, the frequent use of a teacher's red marking pen, and even the way we return assignments or tests.

> "In the right context, a casual remark by a teacher, or even a raised eyebrow or tone of voice can set you on a lifelong journey of discovery or put you off taking even the first step."
>
> —Ken Robinson

Tom was retuning tests he had graded to his math students. After turning Kelsey's test over and flipping it onto her desk, he turned the palms of his hands upward, slapped the sides of his legs, and walked away. After he took a few steps, Kelsey said, "Excuse me, Mr. Cody. Would you mind passing out my test again without all the negative nonverbals?"

Turning back to her, he asked, "Kelsey, would you mind explaining what you just experienced?"

"Well," she said, "I'm not a very good math student but I know that 42% isn't very good. But by the way you passed out my test, threw up your hands, and slapped your pants, you told everyone else in class that I got an F. In fact, by the way you pass out tests, we know what everyone's grades are. Whenever you have eye contact with a student and smile, we know that kid got an A."

Upon realizing that what his student was telling him was true, Tom changed his method for returning test papers. First, he decided to put the grade for the test on the back or the last page. Then he would leave the corrected tests on a table with the student names facing up. Students would pick up their own tests without anyone else knowing their grade.

Whether it's by words, the look or nonverbal gestures, the wolf often communicates publicly that students are stupid or not good enough. Although we would like for our students never to be called these words or experience these nonverbals, eliminating them completely is not going to happen. However, we can empower our students with a strategy for defending themselves when they are called stupid.

Imagine that we also have tucked in our brains an Unequal Sign. The Unequal Sign means 'It doesn't mean I am.' We want our students to know that even though they may be called stupid, it doesn't mean that they are stupid. We can overcome the wolf's intention to have our students believe that they are not smart enough by empowering them to internalize the message of the Unequal Sign. It looks like this:

CALLED ≠ STUPID

It sounds like this: "Even though I'm called stupid, it doesn't mean I am stupid, because stupid doesn't exist."

We want students to internalize this script so that the next time they are called stupid they will think, "No, I'm not. Stupid doesn't exist."

2. Comparison

Comparison is the wolf's primary strategy. When students are compared or when they compare themselves to others, it is highly likely that they will end up feeling or believing that they are not good enough or smart enough.

A surveyed student said, "When I am one of the last people taking the test, I rush through it and don't read the questions or answers." Because other students are completing their tests before she does, this girl is feeling stupid. Just as my reading rate results in me feeling stupid, this student's test taking rate results in her feeling stupid. She is, however, in for a double dose of stupid. Because she doesn't read the questions or answers, she's going to do poorly on the test and feel stupid again when the test is returned to her.

Another student said, "When some of my friends brag about their grades, I tell them my grades are good even though they're not, then think to myself, 'Oh, I'm stupid.'"

School provides constant opportunities for students to compare and judge themselves or for them to be compared or judged by others. Review the countless ways that comparison takes place that are listed on pages 37-39.

It may be that nothing happens more frequently in American middle schools and high schools than comparison and judgment. The question about comparison is not how can we get rid of it. That's not going to happen. Comparison is here to stay. The question is what impact does comparison have on our students, especially when it happens so frequently over such a long time.

A student in a low level math class said, "I feel stupid in this class that nobody else takes. I don't let anyone see that I'm coming into this room." This student actually waited in the hallway outside his classroom until the bell rang for class. Once the hallway was empty, then he went into the classroom. His fear that others would judge his intelligence prevented him from allowing anyone to see the room he was going into. This is a feeling that he experienced every day.

My wife, Paula, considered students in her grade school class to be very smart. Two boys were at the head of the class. "We measured ourselves up to them," she said. Because Paula compared herself to these students, her judgment of herself was that she "wasn't very smart."

I asked her what she could have experienced that would have made a difference for her. "If a teacher would have encouraged my strengths," she said. This finally happened when a teacher read a story about Winnie the Pooh and asked the students to draw a picture related to the story. Paula drew a picture of Winnie the Pooh going up in the air with a red balloon in his hand. Her teacher commented to Paula how well her picture was drawn. Paula remembers 60 years later exactly what her bear looked like and what her teacher said.

When students compare themselves to others or are compared by others, they will take that comparison to one of two places. They will either go to stupid, feeling inadequate or less than someone else, or they will go to learning. Unfortunately, a vast majority of our students will more often take comparison to stupid.

Comparison > Stupid

Comparison > Learning

Imagine being in an art class with Jack, a serious and talented art student. The class is assigned to draw a horse. Jack turns in this picture.

As the picture is mounted for display, you see the smile on the teacher's face and hear the 'wows' and 'aaahhs' from the other classmates.

Your teacher asks for your drawing. As you bring it to the teacher's desk, you are already feeling a bit inadequate.

Upon looking at your picture, the teacher tightens her lips and slightly nods her head back and forth. As she holds up the picture to show the rest of the class, the room is filled with snickers and laughter. In an effort of self-defense, you laugh along with your classmates while wishing that the bell would ring so you could run to the counselors' office and drop the art class. Unfortunately, it's just the beginning of the class as the teacher displays the picture of your horse on the wall...next to Jack's.

Without saying anything out loud, you think to yourself, "This is a stupid assignment. Why do we have to draw horses any way. I'm never going to be an artist. This is a dumb class. And, you know what, Jack, nobody likes you."

The self-talk that just took place in your mind will probably get activated each time you walk into the art room, every time you see your art teacher in the hallway, and whenever you see Jack in the cafeteria. It's likely to be conjured up years later whenever you see a picture of a horse in a magazine or on TV.

In their book *Super Brain*, Deepak Chopra and Rudolph Tanzi comment on the connection between emotion and learning: "Nothing solidifies a memory like emotion….Emotions of joy and wonder, but also of horror and dread, intensify learning. That locks memories in, often for life."[9] Emotions intensifying our students learning math, social studies, and Spanish are a good thing. However, if emotions are locking in the belief that 'I'm not good enough' or 'I'm stupid,' then we have a serious problem that will likely lead to disengagement.

Unfortunately, this comparison scenario is often experienced by our students. For some, it's an every day occurrence. If such is the case, the threat mode in our students gets activated and learning is diminished.

Comparison is not going to be eliminated from American schools. Is there something we can do so comparison doesn't have a negative impact on our students' learning? Yes, we can help our students take comparison to learning. In order for this to happen, comparison needs to become part of our curriculum. **We need to teach students *how* to compare so it leads to learning.** If we don't show them how to do this, it won't happen. They will take comparison to stupid.

Using the art class as an example, a student who has learned how to take comparison to learning might say something like this to Jack, "You did some things in your picture that make the horse look like it's moving. Can you show me how to do that?" Comparison has happened but this student is taking comparison to learning. He's holding up his Unequal Sign and saying: "Even though there's comparison, it doesn't mean I'm stupid, because stupid doesn't exist."

COMPARISON ≠ STUPID

3. Confusion

If comparison is the wolf's primary strategy to get students to feel or believe that they are stupid and not good enough, then confusion is a very close second.

Confusion occurs when students don't understand or know how to do something. A surveyed student said, "I'm confused when guys are talking about stats and football and I have no idea what they're talking about. I usually just don't talk or I pretend I know what they are talking about."

Confusion occurs when students are trying to learn something, but don't get it. Another student said, "I'm confused in school when I don't know the answer. I pretend, blush, and don't raise my hand as much." In both of these examples, we see students beginning to disengage socially and academically.

What are the chances of students in any school being confused on any particular day? Of course, they are very high. It's supposed to be that way. Why?

Confusion is a natural and necessary part of all learning.

All learning begins with not knowing or being confused. If there is no confusion, then there is no learning. The problem is that we have never told students this. So when they get confused, they often go to feeling like there is something wrong with them, that they are stupid or not good enough.

Anything you and I can do today once confused us. If we can ride a bicycle, if we can tie our shoes, if we can add numbers, read, swim, or drive a car, we were once confused about that. But confusion has been given a bad reputation. If we want our students to engage and experience a culture of learning in our schools, we need to change how our students, parents and teachers think about confusion.

The Mountain of Learning

This change can begin to take place by introducing our students to the Mountain of Learning. A mountain is a good metaphor for learning. We start the learning process at the bottom of the mountain where we don't understand something or know how to do something: "I don't get it." Our goal is to climb to top of the mountain where we finally understand or know how to do something: "Aha, I get it." But the only way to get to the top is to pass through the Valley of Confusion. However, if confusion makes us feel stupid, we will go back down the mountain and never have the 'aha' moment.

Kevin actually had this experience in algebra. He started at the bottom of the mountain. He didn't understand algebra, but came to class every day because he wanted to get it. He wanted the algebra 'aha'. All of his previous math experiences dealt with numbers…adding, subtracting, multiplying and dividing. But in algebra class, he experienced letters…like x and y. This didn't make any sense to Kevin. He was confused. Other students in his class seemed to get it, but he didn't. Kevin met the wolf every day in algebra class. He felt stupid and not good enough. Algebra was painful and scary. He wanted to quit. He wanted to go back down the mountain.

This is a common experience for students in American schools, and it begins long before they get to algebra class. However, my grandson Matthew is having a very different experience. He's only one year old. Every day he lies on the floor because that's about all he can do. He sees his siblings and cousins running around the house playing with balls and hitting hockey pucks into nets. Matthew has the thought, "I'd like to be able to do that, but I don't even know how to roll over yet." He's at the bottom of Rollover Mountain. Knowing he wants the rollover 'aha', he starts heading up the mountain. Matthew tries to roll over. He tries to dip one shoulder and get the other one over the top, but he can't quite get it. Matthew's confused.

Matthew's mother is on the floor with him. What will she do? Will she say to him, "Matthew, you're a loser"? No way. Will she compare him to others? "Matthew, your cousins can do this. Why can't you?" I don't think so. There's no wolf in Matthew's life yet. Rather, his mother will smile and encourage. She may even help him roll over, but both of them know that he still hasn't gotten the rollover 'aha'. However, Matthew keeps trying and one day I get pictures and a text message: MATTHEW ROLLED OVER TODAY!!!!!!!

What's the difference between my grandson Matthew and Kevin in algebra class? When Matthew gets to the Valley of Confusion, why does he keep going up the mountain and when Kevin gets to the Valley of Confusion he goes down the mountain? The answer is that my grandson has not yet discovered the Equal Sign. He doesn't equate confusion with stupid. Unfortunately, Kevin has pulled out the Equal Sign and believes that confusion means he's stupid.

If we are Matthew's teacher, our job is to make sure that he never discovers the Equal Sign. If he doesn't, he will keep climbing mountains. In his own unique way, he will experiment with light bulbs and airplanes and, maybe someday, climb the cure-for-cancer mountain.

Our job as teachers is to make confusion normative. Norms are one of the toughest things to combat and change in society. There is no doubt that confusion is normed as something that is bad or something that measures our students as inadequate. We need to make sure our students see confusion in the learning process as natural, necessary, and normal.

After school, Kevin's daughter Cecelia would have a snack and then sit down to do her homework. She would fly through her assignments, but when she got to her math homework, her demeanor, pace, and body language changed drastically. Her willingness to try and her beautiful perseverance that was present just moments before now disappeared.

Recognizing this, Kevin introduced her to the Mountain of Learning. When Cecelia heard that confusion was natural, normal, and necessary, Kevin could see a physical change in her. When he told her that her classmates were more than likely sitting at their kitchen tables feeling confused as well, she relaxed. She understood that she was not alone and that she was not abnormal or stupid. With that realization, she approached her math homework anticipating this wonderful aha moment at the top of the mountain.

Confusion Rocks: Celebrate Confusion

If we want to diminish the wolf's message that confusion means a student is stupid, then we need to send a different message: **Confusion Rocks!!** We need to let our students know that confusion is a cool thing. It's what happens just before we get it and it happens to EVERYONE. If we want our students to keep climbing the mountain once they get confused, we need to find ways to celebrate confusion. Without celebrating confusion, students will have no counter experience to the wolf's message that confusion means stupid and not good enough.

Imagine a student named Isla raising her hand in a social studies class. When called upon, Isla says to her teacher, "We've been discussing the imports and exports of Peru. But I'm confused about how they can even grow some of these products in such a mountainous region."

Giving Isla a look of disapproval, the teacher responds, "You know, Isla, you always seem to be confused. We've been talking about this for two days and we're finished with Peru. Today we are doing a lesson on Argentina so you're going to have to figure out Peru on your own."

Following that public comment from her teacher, Isla will never ask a question again. It's too dangerous. The wolf is now present and prowling in social studies class. Isla is unlikely to learn anything about Argentina. She's heading back down the mountain.

A Top 20 teacher would handle Isla's original question very differently. He would have taught his class the 1-2-3 Clap at the beginning of the year. Whenever he yells out "1-2-3," the class claps once in unison. Then he would say, "Isla, I love that when you don't understand something you ask questions. Class, let's give Isla a 1-2-3 Clap…1-2-3." The class claps once in unison. "So, Isla, I'm going to ask you to sit next to Juanita. Juanita has actually been to Peru. Juanita, please explain the agricultural practices of Peru to Isla. While you are doing that, I'm going to work with this other group. But, Isla, if you still don't understand this after visiting with Juanita, please let me know."

With responses like this, a Top20 teacher keeps Isla engaged in class and the wolf out of his social studies room. Finding creative and meaningful ways of celebrating confusion will keep our students engaged.

COME TO OUR SCHOOL WHERE YOU WILL BE CONFUSED.

Maybe a sign like this in the front of our schools will keep the wolf out of our classrooms.

Students at St. Joseph's School in Imperial, Missouri, see this banner on a wall in their school. At St. Joseph's, confusion is on a pedestal. Confusion doesn't send students back down the mountain. If a second grader is confused about reading, she knows that's why she comes to school. If a fourth grader is confused about fractions, he knows that's why he comes to school.

If we are to be effective teachers for 21st century students, we need to consider two important questions:

1. How am I responding to students when they have been confused?

2. How can I celebrate confusion with my students?

We recently asked a group of 300 high school juniors and seniors if they had ever taken a class in which they already knew everything that was going to be taught, a class in which they would get an 'A' and would not experience confusion. Half of these students acknowledged that they had signed up for such a class.

We thanked them for their honesty and then reminded them that they had wasted their time. Education is not the attainment of A's or the avoidance of confusion. Education only happens when learning happens. If they take a class where there is no confusion, then there is no learning. Remember, confusion is a natural and necessary part of all learning.

We can be of further help to our students by letting them know when confusion is likely to occur in our curriculum. Teaching a short story unit from contemporary American literature wouldn't create a great deal of confusion for our students. The Mountain of Learning is relatively flat. However, during the next unit on Shakespeare's *Hamlet*, the mountain gets much steeper. Letting students know at the beginning of the lesson that confusion will be a constant companion during our climb can encourage them as they experience 16th century English.

If doing what is hard or challenging results in students feeling stupid, they are going to disengage. However, doing what is hard or challenging will not discourage our students as long as the confusion and fumbling that they experience does not equate to stupid or not good enough. If we can keep stupid in the box, our students will keep climbing even the steepest parts of the mountain. They will apply their Unequal Sign and say: "Even though I'm confused, it doesn't mean I'm stupid, because stupid doesn't exist."

CONFUSION ≠ STUPID

4. Can't

The wolf frequently brings stupid into the thoughts and feelings of our students when they can't do something, when they fail or make mistakes. We've covered this previously but let's consider how failure and mistakes apply to students feeling stupid.

A boy gave an example, "When I strike out in a baseball game, I feel that I'm not good at baseball and I'll probably strike out again."

As a youth, Kevin had a baseball experience that mirrors this example. In his first at bat, he hit a shot to right field and raced to first base with a single. His teammates cheered and he was elated. After a few more hits by his teammates, Kevin crossed home plate. As he approached his team's bench, he was met with high fives and smiles.

His second chance to bat went a bit differently. After foul- ing the first pitch, he waited for the pitcher's next offering. When the next pitch came, he swung and missed. Again, he waited. Swinging and missing when the next pitch came, Kevin struck out. With a sinking feeling in his stomach and his head lowered, he walked back to the bench. This time there were no high fives, no smiles or eye contact, and he even heard some groaning. In that moment when he couldn't hit the ball, coupled with his teammates' reactions, he felt stupid and not good enough. Unfortunately, that feeling was unshakable for the entire season.

The wolf had appeared and Kevin suffered from the Ooze Factor. Ooze One means that once stupid sticks to a student, or a player in this case, it spreads to the next time. The next time Kevin stepped up to the plate he was not only holding the bat, he was also holding the feeling of stupid and he struck out again. In fact, his bat never touched the baseball all season.

Kevin was paralyzed by the feeling of stupid that stemmed from not being able to do something (can't). It oozed to each at bat. Strike out followed strike out followed strike out. The wolf of Ooze One was in full swing.

Ooze Two means it spreads to other situations. Because Kevin felt stupid not being able to hit a baseball, he then lacked the confidence to give a speech in English class. Once stupid gets out of the box, it does all sorts of things to mess up our students' lives.

What if Thomas Edison, after failing 12 times trying to invent the light bulb, would have thought, "I'm stupid. I can't do this. This is dumb." We'd still be in the dark. All inventions have been made off the backs of numerous failures and mistakes. If we don't value and learn from mistakes and failures, we'll never have an inventor in our country again.

We sometimes send a message to kids that failure's not an option. But failure is an option...and a good one. Failure and making mistakes are means by which we learn incredible things. So, like confusion, failure and mistakes have to be celebrated. Otherwise, when kids fail or make mistakes, they'll quit trying.

Earlier we mentioned that we need three teachers in every American classroom: a caring adult, mistakes and failure. When these are present, we can combat the preying wolf. If any of these are missing, we don't have a learning culture.

An important part of creating a culture of learning at school is to help parents of students understand, value and celebrate failure and mistakes at home. If we can accomplish that, students will hold up their Unequal Sign when they fail or make a mistake and say: "Even though I can't, it doesn't mean I'm stupid, because stupid doesn't exist."

CAN'T ≠ STUPID

5. Certain situations

Students involved in our research also identified certain situations that made them feel stupid. Some of these situations are related to the first four causes of stupid. They often have to do with being in certain classes or activities or needing help. One student said, "Whenever I have to read out loud in class, I feel stupid."

Earlier we quoted the student who waited in the hallway so his classmates wouldn't see him going into a low-level math class. This boy was a freshman in Tom's pre-algebra class. A girl in this same class said she felt stupid in July when she received her class schedule and realized she was going to be in this lower level class. Should these students be placed in higher-level math classes in order to avoid the feeling of stupid? Obviously not. They are in the right class, but need to experience this class without feeling stupid. They need a Top 20 teacher who will keep stupid in the box. Fortunately, these two students had one.

Tom showed his students that school is a slice of life. School, like the small piece of the pie chart, is a place with a dozen topics. If you're good at those topics, you're considered to be smart. If you're not good at those topics, you're considered to be dumb. But in life there are many things worth knowing and skills worth having and most never have anything to do with subjects covered in school. Remember Glen, my driver who said he wasn't very smart but was good with his hands.

Upon visiting Tom's class, I asked the students: "If Mr. Cody gave a test in Shakespeare, who'd get an A?" I raised my hand. No one else raised their hands. "Who'd get a D or F?" All the students raised their hands. "If Mr. Cody gave a test on automobile mechanics, who'd get a D or F?" I raised my hand. "Who'd get an A?" Three boys raised their hands. So who's stupid, the guy who doesn't know anything about automobile mechanics or the boys who don't know Shakespeare? Neither. **We are different. Everyone has intelligence. We just don't have the same intelligence.**

"For all their popularity and sway over educational policies," claims Ken Robinson, "IQ tests and SATS do not assess the whole range of a student's intellectual abilities. They look for particular sorts of ability….There are considerable pressures for those with strong academic interests. But what about the others, whose real interests or abilities lie elsewhere? For them education has always been an alienating experience."[10]

> "Everybody is a genius. But if you judge a fish by its ability to climb a tree, it will live its whole life believing that it is stupid."
>
> —Albert Einstein

"Human intelligence is much richer," continues Robinson, "than we have been led to believe by industrial/academic education….(It) includes and goes well beyond conventional conceptions of academic ability and IQ."[11]

Wendy Soderman is the founder of IDEAL Elementary and Dream Middle School, an amazing school in Royal Palm Beach, Florida, that I discuss in greater detail in chapter 14. While visiting this school, I noticed that every student seemed to be engaged in every class. During my interview with Wendy, she said, **"Schools determine which kids are smart."** That seems absolutely true. Schools sort kids. Remember, the wolf loves comparing and labeling students. Here are the smart ones and there are the not so smart ones. But then Wendy gave a revolutionary statement: **"My school determines how kids are smart."**

The difference between 'which' and 'how' is incredibly significant and is a major reason why in her school student disengagement is not a problem. Because teachers in Wendy's school use a multiple intelligence format in presenting their lessons, every student at IDEAL School knows that he or she has intelligence. They just are not intelligent in the same way.

Whereas the wolf's goal is to determine which students are smart, we need to help all students discover how they are smart. Dr. Howard Gardner's cognitive research documenting different kinds of intelligence and how people learn, remember, perform, and understand in different ways, can help us with that.[12] The following are the eight different intelligences he has identified.

- Linguistic intelligence ("word smart")
- Logical-mathematical intelligence ("number/reasoning smart")
- Spatial intelligence ("picture smart")
- Bodily-kinesthetic intelligence ("body smart")
- Musical intelligence ("music smart")
- Interpersonal intelligence ("people smart")
- Intrapersonal intelligence ("self smart")
- Naturalistic intelligence ("nature smart")

Ken Robinson argues that we should hesitate "to label someone with high academic abilities as more intelligent than a person with equally high abilities in music or dance....This is not an argument against developing academic abilities: it is *for* an expanded concept of intelligence that includes but also goes beyond them. If we fail to promote a full sense of people's abilities through education and training, some, perhaps most, will never discover what their real capacities are. To that extent they do not really know who they are or what they might become."

Robinson shares a story about meeting a man who wanted to be a fireman since he was in elementary school. When he shared his aspirations with a high school teacher, the teacher told him that he was academically bright and would be wasting his life if he did not go to college. Although he was embarrassed and humiliated by his teacher's response made in front of his friends, the student followed through on his plans to be a fireman. Some years later this fireman saved his teacher's life: "He was in a car wreck and my unit was called out. I pulled him from the car, gave him CPR and saved him. I saved his wife's life, too....I think he thinks better of me now."[13]

Students at the high end of the academic continuum can also develop beliefs that they are stupid. A surveyed student said, "I feel stupid when I'm the first one done with an assignment or test." Why would this be? This student sees herself as the class nerd. Some students who see themselves this way will intentionally perform at a lower level in order to avoid being labeled in a negative way.

Finally, a student said, "I feel stupid when I get 99% on a test. It's not perfect." Students who perform poorly in school or who are in lower level classes can certainly feel stupid, but stupid doesn't discriminate and can also impact students who perform well in school. We need to keep stupid in the box for all students, so they are empowered to hold up their Unequal Sign and say: "Even though there are certain situations, it doesn't mean I'm stupid, because stupid doesn't exist."

CERTAIN SITUATIONS ≠ STUPID

Stupid Destroys Curiosity and Leads to Disengagement

Our students' curiosity is another of the wolf's primary targets. He knows that if he can diminish our students' curiosity, they will disengage in school. When stupid gets out of the box and our students feel or believe they are stupid, curiosity takes a hit.

When students are called stupid, when students are compared, when students are confused, can't do something or have certain experiences that result in their belief that they are stupid, then their curiosity is destroyed and disengagement follows.

If curiosity is so important for engagement, we need to know what it looks like. The face of this student reminds us of what curiosity looks like. He has not yet discovered the Equal Sign. Do you think you could teach this boy? Absolutely.

And here's a picture of a student who has discovered the Equal Sign and has been living with stupid for a long time.

This student, protected by the armor of apathy and the shield of disengagement, even has a sword to take it out on someone else. Is this the dress code in your school? It is for many students in American schools. How likely is it that you can teach this student? That's why we have to keep stupid in the box or get it back in the box once it gets out.

Two young students attended a parent session where we discussed the causes and impact of students feeling stupid and what we can do about it. During the question and answer time, a fifth grade girl said, "Stupid is a myth." A seventh grade boy added, "I came home from school today feeling stupid. Tonight I realized that those were just thoughts that happened in my head. They were not real." Halleluiah!! These two kids are now aware that stupid is something that we make up. That awareness empowers them to keep stupid in the box and fend off the wolf whenever he shows up in their lives. They have moved from fear to conifidence. The job of Top 20 teachers is to help every student move from fear to confidence.

Tips for Keeping Stupid in the Box and the Wolf Out of Our Schools

1. Initiate professional conversations: If we want to disempower the wolf from putting our students in the stupid box, we need to discuss with our colleagues how our students experience stupid and how we can minimize its negative impact.

2. Teach students that stupid doesn't exist: We need to empower students with the Unequal Sign.

3. Make stupid part of the curriculum: We can do this by
   A. Sharing our personal experiences of feeling stupid with our students,

B. Teaching the five causes of stupid,

C. Explaining how comparison can lead to learning,

D. Explaining the importance of 'confusion' in learning and celebrating confusion,

E. Stressing the value of failures and mistakes to learning and growing.

4. Practice the script: We can help students replace unhealthy scripts ("I'm not good enough" or "I'm stupid") with healthier scripts.

   A. Ask students to identify something they do not understand. Then have the entire class say out loud the following sentence. When they come to the blank, they are to say what they don't understand.
   "I am smart. I just don't understand ____ yet."

   B. Ask students to identify something they are confused about. Then have the entire class say out loud the following sentence. When they come to the blank, they are to say what they are confused about.
   "I am smart. I'm just confused about ____."

   C. Ask students to identify something they can't do. Then have the entire class say out loud the following sentence. When they come to the blank, they are to say what they can't do.
   "I am smart. I just can't ____."

5. Help students discover how they have intelligence:
   A. Refer to Dr. Gardner's multiple intelligences.

   B. Have students say, "Wahsoleya" (pronounced wah-so-lay-ya): Wahsoleya is the Lakota Sioux word for 'I am intelligent.' Have students repeat this word or a similar word from a different language when they walk into the classroom and when they leave the classroom.

6. Use a Stupid Box: Decorate a box and put the word 'Stupid' on it. If students are feeling stupid, they can write it on a piece of paper and put it in the box. Example: "I felt stupid during the lesson on fractions." We want  our students to have a sense of power over stupid so they don't dwell on it and allow it to linger inside.

PART 3

ENGAGEMENT 101

CHAPTER NINE

The Fear to Faith Factor

More than anything else, school is a social event in which students are compared and judged. We've seen the myriad of ways by which this happens. The important questions are:

- What is the impact on our students by their being compared and judged for 13 years?

- What effect does being compared and judged from kindergarten through high school have on the inner life of our students?

Ultimately these are unanswerable questions. Since we are concerned about millions of students, the impact of being compared and judged is so diverse that we would never be able to come up with a clear and concise answer. Nonetheless, because the development and expression of the inner life of our students is critical to their own learning and development and to how they relate to others, these questions need to be pursued.

At the risk of being simplistic, I contend that the result of 13 years of being compared and judged is fear. **The continual comparison and judgment that our youth experience in school become a threat to their spirit-to-be. To the extent that this happens, fear diminishes their curiosity, strips away their self-confidence or prevents it from developing, and results in disengagement and unfulfilled potential.**

"From grade school on," says Parker Palmer, "education is a fearful enterprise. As a student, I was in too many classrooms riddled with fear, the fear that leads many children, born with a love of learning, to hate the idea of school....(Our students are) afraid of failing, of not understanding, of being drawn into issues they would rather avoid, of having their ignorance exposed or their prejudices challenged, of looking foolish in front of their peers. When my students' fears mix with mine, fear multiplies geometrically—and education is paralyzed."[14]

To be clear, the wolf dressed in judgment and comparison doesn't show up only in school. He finds our youth at home, through all forms of media, and in whatever social situations they experience. That's why what students experience in school is so terribly important. School can either add to our students' anxiety, worry and loss of self or it can be a primary means for developing self-confidence and discovering true self. Whichever experience our students have will depend on whether or not school is infested with wolves or inhabited by Top 20 teachers.

Although judgment and comparison begin long before our students even come to school and are experienced in the primary and early grades, the big test comes during adolescence. It's during this time in their lives when students are constantly asking:

- Am I smart or dumb?
- Am I good-looking or ugly?
- Am I cool or nerdy?
- Am I a winner or a loser?

As a result, adolescents use their resources not for learning, but to protect their egos. Disengagement becomes a strategic way to protect themselves. Many become full-time members of the No Effort Club where not trying and apathy are badges of honor. It's as if they are hearing adults say, "Now we will measure you and see what you've got," and they respond with "No, you won't."

Nadja Salerno-Sonnenberg is an Italian-born classical violinist, author, and teacher. At the age of 20, she became the youngest-ever prize-winner in the Walter W. Naumburg International Violin Competition. Among her many awards, in 1999 she received the Avery Fisher Prize for outstanding achievement in classical music.[15]

As a young violin student, however, she encountered the wolf: "Ev-

erything I was going through boiled down
to fear. Fear of trying and failing....If you
go to an audition and don't really try, if
you're not really prepared, if you didn't
work as hard as you could have and you
don't win, you have an excuse....Nothing is
harder than saying, 'I gave it my all and it wasn't good enough.'"

> "Fear is everywhere...
> and it cuts us off from
> everything."
>
> —Parker Palmer

Nadja offers another strategy for being invisible: don't try. By not
working hard, students have an excuse for not succeeding. Low effort
is a frequently used strategy when students enter adolescence and
constantly experience comparison and judgment. The low effort syn-
drome is another way to avoid the feeling of not being good enough.
Students feel comfortable and safe when they are in control. Apathy is
a way to maintain that control.

Lauryn Williams is a track and field sprint athlete who competed
internationally for the United States. She won the gold medal in the
100 meter dash at the 2005 World Championships in Athletics. In 2012
she anchored the 4 x 100 meter relay team that won the gold medal
with a world record time at the London Olympics.[16] In other words,
Lauryn runs fast. Imagine being in fifth grade with Lauryn and racing
her during Monday's gym class. Who wins? Lauryn. What if you
raced again on Tuesday? Lauryn wins again. How about Wednesday?
At what point would you say, "I think I'll sit this one out. I'll just hang
out in the bleachers and watch Lauryn run." Of course you would say
that. There's no point in racing Lauryn.

The same thing is happening in fifth grade classrooms where students
have been academically racing classmates for five years. Knowing that
they can't keep up with these 'stars', students begin to sit back and
watch. They disengage from the race: "Nothing is harder than saying,
'I gave it my all and it wasn't enough.'"

Although trying is natural, students aren't foolish. Before students engage by trying, they need to have faith that something good is possible.

Fear or Faith

Within our students' experience of school, **engagement is ultimately determined by fear or faith**. Fear is the emotion that activates the belief that something is not going to turn out okay. Faith or confidence is the belief that we can do it. It's the belief that we will be okay. Fear begins to question faith or confidence. Fear activates the feeling that something is not going to be good. Fear sends a message that we can't do it.

> **Fear** : I won't make it. I won't be okay.
>
> **Faith** : I will make it. I will be okay.

This picture is a good example.

Imagine that you are this skateboarder. Would you go? Are you willing to push off and head down the hill? That will depend on your **fear to faith ratio**. If your fear is greater than your faith, you're not going. You don't think you'll make it. You'd like to try it, but see yourself ending up in the hospital.

But if your faith is greater than your fear, you're going to push off on the skateboard. You feel the thrill of whizzing down the hill and coming to a stop a few feet from the end of the dock.

This same phenomena happens in our students in school.

- Do they ask for help if they don't understand something?
- Do they raise their hand to answer a question?
- Do they introduce themselves to a new student?
- Do they go out for the chess team?
- Do they run for student council?

- Do they sit with different kids during lunch?

- Do they wear something that was given to them for their birthday?

- Do they ask someone out for a date?

- Do they elect to take a certain class?

- Do they volunteer to do an oral report?

- Do they support a student who is being bullied?

The answer to each of these questions will be determined by the fear to faith ratio. The inner voice of our students who experience the wolves of fear and disengagement in school mirrors Little Red Riding Hood's when she says, "As long as I live, I will never leave the path by myself to run into the wood." If this is the inner voice guiding our students, fear will always trump faith. They will disengage and their potential will never be activated.

When I first considered using the story of Little Red Riding Hood as a backdrop for this book, I didn't realize that there was a second part to the story. Red Riding Hood had a second encounter with the wolf.

Some weeks later during another visit to Grandmother, another wolf met Red Riding Hood and tried to entice her from the path. Red Riding Hood, being on her guard, went straight to Grandmother's house and told her that she had met a wolf.

"Well," said Grandmother, "we will shut the door so that he cannot come in."

Soon afterwards the wolf knocked on the door: "Open the door, Grandmother. It's Red Riding Hood and I am bringing you some cakes."

But when the door didn't open, the wolf jumped on the roof, intending to wait until Red Riding Hood went home in the evening. Seeing what the wolf was up to, Grandmother and Red Riding Hood plotted their own strategy.

In front of the house was a great stone trough. Grandmother directed Red Riding Hood: "I made some sausages yesterday. Take the pail and carry the water in which I boiled them to the trough."

Red Riding Hood filled the trough with the water. When the smell of the sausages reached the wolf, he sniffed and peeped down. Stretching out his neck so far, the wolf lost his footing, slipped down from the roof straight into the trough and drowned. Red Riding Hood went joyously home and no one ever did anything to harm her again.

From Red Riding Hood's initial encounter with the wolf, coupled with her experiences with the woodsman, she is able to move from fear to faith. With this in mind, our students can move not only from fear to faith, but from disengagement to engagement. Top 20 teachers can raise their students' faith above their fear to ensure confidence and continued walking on the path of learning.

Let's continue examining the previously asked questions about students' fear and faith in schools. What are the factors that determine our students' fear or faith?

Factors of the Fear to Faith Ratio

Although understanding this ratio that fear trumping faith or faith trumping fear determines our students' willingness to engage might be interesting, it's not of much practical value. However, if we could better understand what causes the fear or faith, we might be able to influence the ratio in ways that benefit our students. If we could minimize the fear and enhance our students' faith or confidence, then we can have a direct impact on reducing our students' disengagement and increasing their engagement.

What factors in school cause fear or faith in our students?

When we consider what students experience in school and how it impacts their inner life, seven factors can be identified as causes of fear or faith.

1. Teachers
2. Classmates
3. Parents
4. Content
5. Processes
6. Results or Outcomes
7. Mistakes and Failures

Although we will focus on each of these factors separately, they are not always independent of each other. Each factor provides a means by which the wolf (fear) and the Top 20 teacher (faith) make themselves present in the lives of students.

Fear to Faith Factor 1: Teachers

Teachers are tremendously important in students' lives. Other than family members, probably no other person plays a more important role in a students' development than teachers. How teachers relate to students has a powerful impact on whether or not students like school and stay engaged in learning. In both positive and negative ways, what teachers say and do have a lasting impression on students. Although it happened more than 55 years ago when I was in the fifth grade, I still remember a teacher calling me a coward by saying, "You have a yellow streak down your back."

> "(T)eachers possess the power to create conditions that can help students learn a great deal—or keep them from learning much at all."
>
> —Parker Palmer

Haim Ginott clearly illustrates the influence a teacher possesses: "As a teacher I possess tremendous power to make a child's life miserable or joyous. I can be a tool of torture or an instrument of inspiration. I can humiliate or humor, hurt or heal. In all situations, it is my response that decides whether a crisis will be escalated or de-escalated, and a child humanized or de-humanized."[17]

Although students have countless images and impressions of teachers, most images or impressions fall into the categories of judge or coach (ally). It's understandable why students would view teachers as judges. Judging is largely what teachers do. They judge their students' performance, learning, ability, attitude, behavior, thinking, motives, potential, intelligence and character. Teachers mark what their students do as being right or wrong (with a red pen), good or bad, mature or immature. They reward and punish. Teachers also let other people know their judgments. They fill out report cards and conference with colleagues and parents. Teachers determine standards and make the final call on whether or not students 'pass' or 'fail'. As such, teachers have a great deal of power over their students' lives and what students think about themselves.

Teachers can also be viewed as coaches or allies. Students see their teachers as someone helping them learn or improve at something. Teachers listen, understand, support and care. They are someone students depend on, admire, trust and respect. They see teachers as being kind, patient, friendly and dedicated to their growth and development. Teachers are safe.

Within these two roles, teachers cause or reduce fear or faith in students. We asked 85 high school freshmen how teachers did this. These are students from Tom's Thinking, Learning and Communicating class. Since we will be sharing their opinions during the remainder of this chapter, we will refer to them as the student panel. They responded by sharing the following ways they experience teachers causing or reducing fear.

Teachers cause fear by:

Yelling

Calling on me when I don't want to be called on or don't have an answer

Turning attention just on me

Singling me out

Telling my test scores or grades to others

Embarrassing me

Giving me the look when I ask a question that everyone knows

Not wanting to help me

Criticizing

Writing 'See me' on a test

Calling students up to the board

Not making sure I understand the material

Making body gestures

Not caring about my life

Asking me in front of the class to come in for extra help

Teachers reduce fear by:

Being calm, patient and sympathetic

Being willing to slow down

Encouraging us to ask questions

Leaving me alone when I'm having a bad day

Helping me understand the material I am learning or when I'm lost

Letting me know it's okay to make mistakes

Celebrating mistakes

Keeping my test scores private

Calling on me when my hand is raised

Getting to know me, asking about my life and being able to relate to my life

Saying: "Try again, but here's a way you can improve."

Asking if I want to read out loud or if I feel like going up to the board

Comforting me when I get something wrong

Complimenting failure

Praising me in front of the class

Trying different ways to talk to me

Remembering my name

In simplest terms, these two lists can be boiled down to humiliate or help. Students are more likely to experience humiliation when teachers are in the judge role and help when teachers are in the coach role. Humiliation leads to disengagement and help leads to engagement.

Although teachers at times can intentionally humiliate students, I tend to believe that most of the time when students feel humiliated it is not what teachers intend. Nonetheless, we need to be aware that we are more likely to cause humiliation or fear when we are in the judge role. Consequently, can we say or do things in this role that minimizes fear? One possibility is to attach a 'coaching' statement after a 'judging' statement.

> "I see that you didn't do well on this test. Let's find some time to go over this so you have a better understanding of this material."

> "I think the mistakes you made on this assignment occurred because you weren't listening when I gave instructions. I just want to make sure you learn something from that."

Fear to Faith Factor 2: Classmates

Classmates are significant ways that the wolf and woodsman show up in school. Like teachers, classmates can also fill the roles of judge or coach by humiliating or helping. Students can view their peers as a threat simply because they are better at the subject being taught or the activity being conducted. When students compare themselves to classmates, they frequently conclude that they are not good enough. Peers can be more intentional in causing this feeling by bullying, laughing or verbal comments that are cruel or demeaning.

But classmates are also a major enjoyment for students in school. Connecting with friends is something many students enjoy most about their school day.

When asked how classmates cause or reduce fear, our freshman student panel responded with the following.

Classmates cause fear by:

Mocking, making fun, teasing or insulting

Judging

Making me feel unwanted

Being rude

Laughing and making jokes

Calling names

Gossiping, spreading rumors and creating drama

Bullying and intimidating

Being smart or getting amazing grades

Pointing out something I did wrong

Rolling eyes over my intelligence

Judging me so I can't be myself

Telling someone they are not good enough

Classmates reduce fear by:

Complimenting

Talking to me

Being kind when I make a mistake

Accepting me for who I am

Treating me with respect

Being friendly, supportive, and nice

Helping me learn when I'm struggling with something

Encouraging

Critiquing me in a way that will help me and not make me feel worse

Not judging

Telling kids to stop laughing

Giving everyone a chance

Listening and understanding

Being patient

Helping with problems

Not comparing grades

Celebrating people's different abilities

Laughing with me

Not bragging

The interesting thing about this second list is that everything these ninth graders said is really quite easy to do. In other words, classmates have ready access to power to make a positive difference in how peers experience school.

I experienced an example of this simple yet profound power on the first day of my freshman year in high school. Being one of only two students from my grade school who went to this high school, I didn't know many other students in my class. I did know Jody Koehler, a kid I had played basketball against in grade school. I was fumbling with the combination of my locker before first hour class when Jody walked up to me. We chatted briefly and then, after telling me that we had first hour class together, he said, "I'll save you a seat." Jody said those five words to me 52 years ago and I still remember them today.

I don't think I can remember anything that was said to me yesterday, yet I can remember what was said to me 52 years ago. How is that possible? It has to do with vulnerability. Being a freshman on the first day of school when I didn't know anyone was the condition that made me vulnerable. Would I make it in this new school? Would I be accepted? Would I have friends? Would I make the basketball team? Would I ever be able to get into this stupid locker? Would I get to my class on time? Would I remember my schedule? In the midst of all of that confusion, a woodsman named Jody showed up and with five simple words put much of my anxiety at ease.

With this in mind, one of the most powerful untapped resources we have in schools is older students. These would include juniors and seniors in high school or students in the upper grades in grade school or middle school. These are students who 'know the ropes'. They are, for the most part, already established socially. They know how to open their lockers and where the boys or girls bathrooms are. They understand the teachers and what is expected in their classes. These are woodsmen and woods-women in waiting.

Tom now has older students, called student mentors, working with him in all of his classes. They function as mentors for the younger students. They are a voice of wisdom who can connect easily to Tom's students. They advocate for the younger kids and even remind Tom when he is acting as a wolf. A ninth grader in Tom's math class did only two problems when the assignment sheet said #9-31. He did just

#9 and #31. The student mentor stopped Tom from intervening as a wolf and said, "I've got this one." Taking the kid out into the hall, the mentor saved the confused ninth grader and the entire learning environment in Tom's room.

Tom's student mentors work with kids who appear to be lonely, sad or disconnected socially. They approach students who appear to be disengaged in class and gently remind them of their power to focus more effectively. They even offer Tom insights about younger students that he would not have considered. Being a perfect blend of maturity and credibility, these older students are effective woodsmen and woods-women for vulnerable younger students.

Although students can be a powerful support for each other, Leah's story is an example of classmates who show up as the wolf.

> I waited with anticipation at the corner for my best friend Patti to walk the final block to school for the start of our fifth grade year. I walked that final block feeling both excited and nervous for the day to get underway. This was the same feeling I had at the beginning of each new school year. Ever since kindergarten, school had been a positive place to learn and to be with my friends. I was a well-adjusted, happy, confident girl who was ready to learn.
>
> Mrs. Nash met us at the door and we found our desks near one another in the U-shaped formation. Two new girls, who were joining our fifth grade class, were introduced to us. They came from two different schools and the possibility of making new friends was exciting to me.
>
> The first week of school was normal. We all seemed to be coming together as a group. But then something shifted. As the first month came to an end, the possibilities and excitement I felt on that first day waned. The two new girls had formed a bond and began to exclude the other girls in the class. Being one of the more popular, smart, and athletic girls, I soon became an obvious threat to them.

It started slowly. First a comment about what I was wearing. Next their little group whispered softly and laughed as I walked toward them. Then notes with mean statements were passed to my desk and laughter as I answered a question or tried to complete a problem at the board. It became a daily barrage of ridicule and exclusion. I showed up as a fifth grader very open, ready to learn, and confident in my abilities. By the end of the first month I became a student who was hesitant, withdrawn and wishing I could just disappear.

I was no longer concerned or interested in learning. I was only interested in protecting myself from further hurt, embarrassment and shame. In school, the previous days lesson is a building block to each new concept and idea being taught. Because I was only concerned with survival, I was no longer building that foundation of what I needed to know so I could learn what would come next. This compounded the issue for me. I became terrified to hear my name called. Being called to the board to publicly demonstrate my ability by completing a math problem or diagraming a sentence became just another way for the students in my class to harass and ridicule me. When I didn't know how to do something, it was later used against me.

I quickly learned that if I wanted to survive I had to avoid being seen. I walked through the school door every morning and became invisible. I became consumed with how to stay out of the light so others wouldn't see me and avoided bringing any attention to myself. My only concern was in knowing where the other girls were, what was being said, who was laughing at what and where the next hit would come from.

The deeper and more damaging issue was that in my heart I knew that I didn't understand the content that was being taught. I hadn't learned it because I wasn't focused on learning. I was focused only on survival. I didn't have any way to challenge what they were saying about me, because I believed

> it was true. Therefore, there must be something fundamental-
> ly wrong with me. I became locked into the belief that I was
> stupid. There was no place for me. I had no worth.

Although these deep-rooted beliefs that she was stupid and lacked any inherent worth started in the fifth grade, Leah carried them to high school where she met three life-saving woodsmen.

Mr. Tenney was her high school choir teacher. Choir was the one class where she didn't have to hide but could show up and be herself. Mr. Tenney intentionally made Leah feel seen and valued. He created a safe place for her to belong. He challenged the long-held beliefs that Leah had about herself. Being gifted with the ability to sing, the stupid feeling Leah had in every other class didn't present its ugly head when she walked into choir.

Coach Dybevik, her basketball coach, and Coach Muir, her softball coach, also created a place of belonging for Leah. Being a gifted athlete, Leah contributed to her teams' success and felt welcomed by her teammates. More importantly, her coaches were concerned about more than her athletic ability. They believed in Leah and reminded her on a daily basis that her worth didn't come from her performance. This was in direct opposition to everything she felt and believed about her academic courses and abilities.

These three men were the glue that connected Leah to school. They were the reason she showed up in the morning to struggle through the day, the reason she went in to get extra help from teachers, the reason she tried to learn, and ultimately the reason she was able to graduate from high school and college. They demonstrate the power of a Top 20 teacher in overcoming the fear generated by the wolf and keeping a student engaged in learning and keeping alive her spirit-to-be.

Fear to Faith Factor 3: Parents

Although parents are not in school, their opinions, expectations or concerns about what their sons and daughters are doing or accomplishing have an impact on students during school. Like teachers and class-mates, parents also play the roles of judge or coach. The wolf or woods-man shows up based on how parents respond to school matters.

- Do parents attend parent/teacher conferences?
- Do parents take an interest in what their children are doing in school?
- Do parents compare one child to another?
- Do parents encourage curiosity in their children?
- Do parents demonstrate the importance of learning in their own lives?
- How do parents perceive grades and test scores?
- How do parents respond to their children's mistakes or failures?
- How are parents expressing praise?
- How are parents involved with their children's homework?

As mentioned earlier, some of my grandchildren attend school across the street from our home. After picking up her four children at the end of the school day recently, our daughter Molly brought the kids to our house. As soon as they came in, they started doing their homework. That routine in their family has established a habit in our grandchil-dren and sends a message that learning is important.

I have worked with students and teachers in several Native-American schools on reservations. I am in awe of the traditional culture of these people and their efforts to maintain their cultural values in the young-er generation. Unfortunately, some of the elders in these communities experienced painful and degrading school experiences when they were children. Often taken from their homes and placed in boarding schools away from their families, they were stripped of their native language, dress, traditions and values. In school they encountered one wolf after another. In various degrees, the suffering that these elders experienced in school still has an impact on their grandchildren. The importance of school and the distrust of school sometimes mix in an unclear message sent to the younger generation.

Our student panel shared opinions of how parents can cause or reduce fear.

Parents cause fear by:

Yelling at me for grades

Threatening for bad grades

Not leaving me alone

Telling me I'm wrong all the time

Not listening to my opinions

Having high and unrealistic expectations

Being overly concerned about grades and bugging me about my grades

Creating pressure

Not understanding me

Making everything so serious

Comparing me to someone else

Saying that they are disappointed in me

Saying, "You can do better than that."

Telling me that something is easy and I should get an A

Not seeing things from my point of view

Parents reduce fear by:

Being calm

Being sympathetic, understanding and supportive

Accepting that I'm doing my best

Encouraging

Listening

Letting me know that as long as I am trying my hardest that things will be okay

Helping with what I need help on

Not comparing me to others

Talking to me before they blow up

Loving me

Explaining things

Trusting me and giving me freedom

Celebrating the good that I do

Saying, "I have faith in you."

In their own words, these students seem to be repeating what was stated earlier: human being precedes human doing. In order to experience their own worth, they need to know that their parents see them as worthy. Our students' confidence in themselves is often the by-product of the confidence someone else has had in them. Kevin is an example of this.

Kevin's grades and performance in school from a young age rarely showcased his true potential. School was difficult for him. Because he had received and internalized the message that he was not smart enough and at times deemed himself to be stupid, his level of engagement was minimal.

Fortunately for Kevin, his parents were a constant and loud chorus of voices saying otherwise. His parents continually told him that he was not only smart, but also able to handle the academic challenges that came his way. When Kevin and his older sister would get into fights, they called each other names and hurt each other's feelings. However, two words were off limits: stupid and dumb. Kevin's parents forbid those two words knowing the incredible power they can have over young people. Their confidence in Kevin trumped his feelings of stupid and not being smart enough. They were a constant stream of encouragement and served as a safe reminder that he could be successful. As a result, Kevin is a confident adult who is comfortable in his own skin. Consequently, he is able to be a source of encouragement to his own children and students.

Fear to Faith Factor 4: Content

Content refers to what is being taught or presented in various subject areas. Traditionally, these would include math, English or language arts, social studies, science, foreign language, art, music, physical education, computer science and a wide range of elective subjects. For students, the wolf shows up in content that is generally more difficult. When it's 'hard', students are more likely to disengage. For some students, entire subjects are more stressful than others. Math, because it includes new material every day that tends to become more challenging, is the subject most often identified by students in this way.

However, 'hard' and 'easy' also apply to content within a subject. As mentioned earlier, as a high school English teacher, a short story unit didn't cause as much trepidation in students as Shakespeare's *Hamlet*. Nor did writing a paragraph create as much anxiety as a term paper.

Every subject area has both easier and more challenging parts for students.

Here is what our student panel said about content that causes or reduces fear.

Content causes fear when it:

Is hard to understand or confusing	Is something I don't like
Results in my having no idea what we are talking about	Is presented in a way that is overly concerned about points or grades
Includes pop quizzes or tests	Is in a class where I sit by people I don't know
Has no relevancy in my life	
Is difficult or challenging	Is taught a lot at once...monumental amounts
Involves reading or math	Gets harder and harder

Content reduces fear when it:

Is material I already know so I don't have to study	Is something I can get into
Is something I like	Is in a class where I can sit by people I know
Is relevant and we can use it in life	Is planned well
Is easy and simple	Is manageable
Is explained well	Is more physical
Is something I understand	Is not going too fast
Is fun or creative	Goes slower through harder stuff

The panel makes it quite simple. Fear or frustration is caused by content that is difficult. If that's the case, should we only teach students content that is easy? Obviously not. However, we have to consider how best to prepare our students for doing what is difficult.

When my granddaughter Caroline was in third grade, I coached her basketball team. At the beginning of the first practice, I had the girls sit in a circle on the floor. "Raise your hand," I said, "if you want to get better at basketball." All ten third graders raised their hands. "There's only one way to do that," I added. "You have to do what's hard. If we only practice what you can already do, that would be easy, but you wouldn't get better. So we have to practice what you're not so good at. This will be hard and you will make lots of mistakes, but we'll get better. Let's start getting better right now. Each of you get two basketballs and start dribbling two balls at the same time."

As soon as these young players began the drill, balls started rolling in every direction. They'd scamper after their ball and try again. Throughout this five minute drill, I kept yelling, "You're getting better. You're getting better." Although they were struggling, they kept trying. Were the girls feeling frustration? Yes, but not one of them said, "This is too hard." Since the girls knew that the drill was going to be challenging, they were better prepared to handle the wolf of frustration when he appeared.

I have done this drill with other young basketball players without introducing it the way I did with these third graders. In those situations, I would immediately hear them say, "I can't do this. This is hard." Why the difference? I hadn't made the connection for these kids that hard was necessary if they wanted to get better. I hadn't made the connection that making mistakes trying to do something that they couldn't easily do was a sign that they were getting better.

If we are going to teach a challenging part of our curriculum, we can keep the wolf at bay by letting our students know that this is a way to get better. Furthermore, we need to let them know that they will not only be improving at dribbling a basketball, reading difficult literature, or writing prose, but they will also be getting better at dealing with adversity, which is important in every facet of their lives.

If you can only do what's easy, you can only do what's easy.

If you can do what's hard, you can do what's easy and you can do what's hard.

Fear to Faith Factor 5: Processes or Class Activities

Whereas **content is what** is being taught, **processes are how** it is being taught. Processes impact students differently. For some, they are means by which the wolf shows up.

Tom is a math genius. He can calculate the square root of five figure numbers in his head. I did okay in math and can tell you the square root of 144. After that I need a calculator. Imagine if we had been in the same eighth grade math class and the teacher asked us to go up to the board and work on a math problem. As I am walking to the board, I am thinking, "You've got to be kidding me. This is going to be embarrassing. It's going to take me five minutes to figure this out. Tom will be done in 30 seconds. This is stupid and I'm so dumb at math." Meanwhile, as Tom's walking to the board, he's thinking, "The answer is 4x(3y+z)." He's written the answer on the board and is back to his seat before I pick up the marker. My brain goes into survive mode as I turn to the teacher and say, "Mrs. Johnson, can I go to the bathroom?" That, of course, is followed by a chorus of laughter coming from my classmates.

Processes will be considered in greater detail in chapter 10, but let's see what our freshman panel says about processes causing or reducing fear.

Processes (class activities) cause fear when:

They are complicated, difficult or confusing	They involve public speaking
I am called out in front of people	I have to get out of my comfort zone
I have to stand in front of the class	They are pointless or boring
They are poorly explained	I have to share my ideas with the class
They put people on the spot	I have to read aloud
I am being laughed at when giving the wrong answer	We have to do stuff on the board
	They involve tests and quizzes

Processes (class activities) reduce fear when:

They are straight forward and simple	They allow for a variety of ways to learn
I am being helped	
They are easy	They are fun and interactive
They are helping everyone so we don't feel stupid	They are safe
	I am really understanding what we are doing
We are working in groups or with partners	They take into account how I think
We are not being put on the spot	They involve more physical movements

What makes teaching so difficult is that the same process or class activity that creates confidence for some students creates fear and anxiety for others.

Fear to Faith Factor 6: Results or Outcomes

Results or outcomes refer to what students get from their participation or involvement. Remember hearing this question in school, "Whadya get?" Unfortunately, the only answer I can ever recall being given to that question was a score or a grade. That's still true today. We have focused on grades and test scores rather than learning and development of qualities and skills.

At a very young age our students find the wolf present in grades. When Kevin asked his fourth grade daughter about fear in school, she immediately started reliving report cards where minuses (-) were present in the math category. When his daughter knows a big math test is coming up, she often thinks back to those minuses, enabling the fear from the wolf to grow and get in the way of true preparation and learning for the upcoming assessment.

This exclusive focus on grades is reflected by our student panel's comments about how outcomes and results cause or reduce fear.

Results or outcomes cause fear when:

I get bad grades	They are embarrassing
They cause pressure	They are less than an A-
I'm being grounded	They're all about tests
I fail	I get down on myself
I don't understanding why I get a bad grade	There's negative criticism
	Others are told about my grade

Results or outcomes reduce fear when:

I'm in an easy class	Grades are not read out to the class
There's no pressure	I've already learned it
I get good grades	Help is offered
I am encouraged	I get tips on how to improve
They are greater than B+	I know in advance when tests are coming so I can study
They allow for extra credit	

Chapter 11 will focus more on the question of "Whadya get?"

Fear to Faith Factor 7: Mistakes and Failure

We have seen in chapter 7 how mistakes and failure are frequent and necessary experiences if learning and human development are going to occur. We've also seen how these experiences provide opportunities for the wolf to salivate over us like red meat. Teacher, classmate and parent responses to students when they fail or make mistakes leave students with experiences that range from humiliation and fear to learning and growth. Based on how students experience failure and mistakes, they will be more or less willing to move outside their Comfort Zone. When fear of making mistakes takes over, our students are more likely to avoid the wolf by staying safely tucked inside their Comfort Zones, which unfortunately prevents opportunities to learn. These possibilities are clearly illustrated by our freshman panel's responses to how mistakes and failure cause or reduce fear.

Mistakes and Failure cause fear when:

I'm ridiculed or embarrassed	I wonder what people think of me
People make fun of me	I can't come back from failures
They make me upset or mad	They are done in public
I am judged	There are consequences
I don't know how to do a problem	I worry about looking foolish
They are made into a big deal	I make the same mistake again
Others point out my mistakes	

Mistakes and Failure reduce fear when:

I learn from mistakes	Comfort is offered
They are not pointed out	It doesn't matter
I am encouraged when I make a mistake	Someone say, "It's ok, you're getting there. I'll help you."
I know exactly what I'm supposed to do	I am understood
	I tell myself I'm okay
I am helped after the mistake	I'm shown that we all make mistakes
Making mistakes is seen as a good thing	Mistakes are celebrated

Whether or not we develop a culture of learning in our classrooms is largely determined by how our students experience mistakes and failure.

The Fear to Faith Equation

These seven factors offer us a means for measuring the fear or faith experienced by students. The expressed or imagined opinions of teachers, classmates and parents (OPOs of T + Cl + P), the content that is being taught (C), the processes being used (Pr), the results or outcomes students get (R), and how students are responded to when they make mistakes or fail (M/F) provide a formula for the amount of fear or faith students experience.

$$\text{Fear or Faith} = \text{OPOs} (T + Cl + P) + C + Pr + R + M/F$$

Obviously fear or anxiety and faith or confidence cannot be measured in any exact way. However, this formula can be considered as an inexact tool for better understanding the degree to which students are experiencing fear or faith.

Let's consider examples of how two students on our freshman panel used the equation to assess their level of fear and faith in the math class they were currently taking. We'll call one student Tim and the other student Emma. Each assessed the seven factors ranging from a great amount of fear (-5) to a great amount of faith (+5) according to the following continuum.

Fear	-5	-4	-3	-2	-1	+1	+2	+3	+4	+5	**Faith**

Fear — Worry ... Faith — Peace of mind
Anxiety/Stress ... Calm/Relaxed
Doubt ... Confident
Dread ... Excitement
Avoid ... Look forward to
"I'm not going to make it." ... "I'm going to make it."
"It's not going to be ok." ... "It's going to be ok."

	Tim	Emma
Teacher	-3	+4
Classmates	-4	+1
Parents	-2	+3
Content	-3	+4
Processes	-4	-1
Results	-2	+4
Mistakes/Failure	-4	+4
Total	-22	+19

When asked to explain their total numbers, Tim shared that his teacher would often call on him when he didn't know the answer (T), half of his classmates were math nerds (Cl), his parents wondered why he wasn't doing as well as his sister who had taken the same class (P), math had always been hard for him (C), he hated having to go up to the board (Pr), a C- grade seemed unfair (R), and kids who made mistakes were ridiculed (M/F). Tim expressed feeling anxious every day he walked into this room.

Emma's teacher was also her volleyball coach for whom she enjoyed playing (T), some students in the class were better at math than she was, but three of her best friends were in the class and they often did their math assignments together during lunch or after practice (Cl), her parents were proud of how responsible she was about getting her homework done (P), math had always been one of her favorite classes (C), she was reluctant to present her work publicly (Pr), she felt that math was helping her think clearly and be more logical (R), and mistakes in class were encouraged as long as students learned from them (M/F). Emma often walked into math class with a smile and frequently stayed after class to talk with her teacher.

Tim and Emma are having drastically different experiences in math. Tim's level of fear and lack of faith not only impacts him while he is in class, but also take over his mental state before and after class. Emma, on the other hand, has a high level of faith, which in turn lowers her feelings of fear. She is thriving and able to navigate the learning environment with confidence, feelings of safety and belonging, and is in a state of mind where learning can occur.

If we want our students to be engaged in learning, we need to understand how they experience fear in our classroom. By having their students use the fear or faith assessment tool in their classroom, Top 20 teachers can identify if their students' fear may be trumping faith or vice versa. With this awareness, teachers can address those areas in ways that elevate the feelings of faith and diminish the feelings of fear. When this occurs, student engagement will increase.

CHAPTER TEN

Classroom Processes: Creating Safe Connections That Foster Student Engagement

One of the many tools in a teacher's toolbox is classroom processes, the ways lessons are presented and the ways students participate in order to attain learning. These include:

Student-led discussion	Lecture	Group reading
Spelling bee	Silent reading	Games
Kinesthetic activities	Use of manipulatives	Role play
Cooperative activities	Work at the board	Movies
Student presentations	Small group	Speech
Questioning	Creative dramatics	Technology

Although they may vary based on the age of students, classroom processes are intended to engage students in learning. Given the focus of this book, classroom processes need to be examined for wolf prints. Are the processes we are using to help students learn influencing their engagement or disengagement?

What makes teaching so difficult is that the same process can impact students differently. A teaching process might engage some students in learning while disengaging others. Let's consider how this might happen even for adults.

During our presentations to teachers, we tell them that we are going to have a group spelling bee. We explain that we will divide the group into teams and that each team member will be given a word to spell. Correctly spelled words yield one point for their team; incorrectly spelled words equal no team points.

After giving these directions, we ask the teachers if anyone would like to find some way to excuse himself from this activity. Does anyone want to say, "I have a dentist appointment and have to leave now"? We always get a few participants who prefer not to participate in the spelling bee. We also ask if anyone is excited to participate in this activity. A few respond that they are looking forward to the spelling test. What we have discovered is that regarding this one process (a spelling bee) some people experience fear and would like to disengage while others experience confidence and can't wait to get started.

We can drill down a bit deeper and better understand what is really taking place in this situation. Participants came into this presentation with a belief about themselves as either a good or poor speller. Although they came with that belief, they were not conscious of that belief until we said we would be conducting a spelling bee. At that moment, their belief of themselves as a speller was activated. Some participants felt fear or anxiety and wanted to find a way out while others felt confident and fully engaged.

What we can learn from this example is that all students enter our classrooms with numerous beliefs about themselves...beliefs about whether they are good or bad at fractions, good or bad at reading, good or bad at art or singing, good or bad at jumping rope, dribbling a basketball or hitting a tennis ball. When we announce what we are going to be doing in class that day, their beliefs get activated and, in that moment, they want to either engage or disengage. The determining factor is whether or not students sense a threat coming from the lesson's content or processes. If so, the survive mode of their brain turns on and the thrive mode shuts down.

Relative to potential threat, turtles and possums might be good examples of what happens in the classroom to disengaged students. When a turtle senses a threat, it tucks itself inside its shell. When a possum sense a threat, it plays dead. Disengagement, an act of self-defense for turtles and possums, occurs when their environment isn't safe. Student disengagement occurs for the same reason. Students sense that their environment is not safe. Their decision to disengage or disappear is an effort to self-defend. Realizing this, Top 20 teachers limit disengagement by creating a safe environment with safe connections.

Three Principles of Engagement

Understanding the basic functions of their students' brains, Top 20 teachers know that by creating a safe environment their students' thrive mode will remain active. Top 20 teachers create safety and foster engagement by practicing (1) three principles of engagement, (2) implementing processes of engagement, and (3) fostering a classroom and school-wide culture of safety (to be covered in Chapter 12).

Let's first consider three principles of engagement.

1. Name Matters: A student's name identifies her. The longer a student's name is not heard in our classroom, the more likely she will be disengaged. When we speak the names of our students, we acknowledge their existence and their presence in the room. We make contact with their identity and who they are. That acknowledgement and that contact make it more likely for students to be engaged in whatever we are doing and less likely for students to disappear. Name matters. When students' names are part of our processes, they will more likely be engaged.

2. Voice Matters: The longer a student's voice is not heard in our classroom, the more likely he will be disengaged. When a student's voice is spoken, he is acknowledging presence. He is essentially saying, "I am here now." Voice matters. When our processes involve students' voices being spoken, they will more likely be engaged.

3. Belonging Matters: When we come into a room of people, we normally choose to sit next to someone we know, someone with whom we have a connection. We seldom choose to approach those we don't know when we can approach someone we do know. Think of how this happens at parties we attend. What's true for us is also true for students.

If we stand outside a middle school or high school as students are leaving the building at the end of the day, they are either walking with a friend or texting a friend. Why is this? Belonging matters. The more we can create a sense of belonging in our processes, the more likely students will be engaged.

The three principles of name, voice and belonging relate to our students as human beings. When they sense

> "We know that fear fades when people meet the stranger and learn not only that the stranger lacks horns but may even come bearing gifts."
>
> —Parker Palmer

that it is safe to be a human being, when they experience a connection with other human beings, they are more likely to engage, to be human doers, to come out of their shells and not pretend to be invisible.

Implementing Processes of Engagement

If the processes we use incorporate these three principles of engagement, our students are more likely to engage in learning. Let's consider two classroom processes that incorporate the three principles of engagement: Pods and 4-at-the-Door.

Pods is a process that has four students participate in small group discussions about any question or topic we might be covering in class. Detailed directions for conducting Pods are provided on page 222 in the Appendix.

The purpose of Pods is to create a learning culture by enhancing the group experience, having every student's voice and name matter and developing a sense of belonging and connection. Pods utilize the above-mentioned principles of engagement through the assigning of the following roles to each of the four students:

- **Asker**: the student responsible for re-asking the teacher's discussion question to the other students in the Pod.

- **First Responder**: the student assigned to be the first one to answer the discussion question.

- **Scribe**: the student responsible for recording the name of the students and their answer to the question.

- **Voice**: the student who will share the Pod's recorded answers with the rest of the class.

These four assigned roles are designed to implement the principles of name matters, voice matters, and belonging matters. Pods help to create a sense of safety in which students are more likely to engage.

While doing research for this book, I visited one of Tom's classes. I explained to his freshmen students what my book was about and then asked them if they could share with me examples of how they have experienced fear in school. My request fell on deaf ears. The room was totally silent; no hand was raised. Then Tom said to his students, "Go into your Pods and talk about Mr. Bernabei's question." In the safety of their Pods, students freely shared numerous examples of experiencing fear in school.

Sometimes the wolf appears in large groups, especially when more personal issues are being discussed and greater vulnerability is required. However, in a Pod group of four where safety and connections have been established, students are at ease in sharing their opinions or experiences. Over time, the sense of safety students feel in the small Pod group can transfer to the larger full class group.

Pods is just one of numerous processes teachers can use to engage students in class discussions. The purpose in sharing Pods here is simply to consider the effect of various processes we use with our students. Does a process that we are using:

- Engage some students but not others?
- Incorporate a student's name and voice and help to establish belonging?
- Result in some students feeling compared or judged, less than or not good enough?

4-at-the-Door

Earlier I mentioned Wendy Soderman and her school in Royal Palm Beach, Florida. During my first visit to IDEAL School, I stopped in every classroom. The first student I met was Billy. When I walked into his classroom, this little boy came up to meet me at the door and said, "Good morning, my name is Billy. Welcome to IDEAL School. Do you have any questions?"

Looking down at Billy, I asked, "Where am I?"

"You're at IDEAL School," said Billy with confidence. "Do you have any other questions?"

What this young boy taught me was the importance of what happens at the door to a classroom.

When I began teaching in 1970, if you asked me what the purpose of the door to my room was, I would have said that it was an opening in the wall so students could come in the room and have me pour Shakespeare into their heads. Oh my, was I ever missing it. The door may be the most important part of a classroom. What happens or doesn't happen there can determine classroom culture and cause students to engage or disengage. I learned that from Billy.

Billy taught me what has become a regular part of our teacher training: 4-at-the-Door. It begins with teachers meeting their students at the door to their classroom, not sitting at their desk or checking emails. They are meeting their students at the door with four greetings.

1. Name-to-name: As a student enters our classroom, we say, "Good morning, Megan," and she says, "Good morning, Mr. B." The first thing our students hear in our room is their name. Name matters. When we say their name, we identify and recognize their existence as a human being. Remember, they enter as human beings before they become human doers.

2. Eye-to-eye: When students enter our classroom, our attention is immediately on them. We make eye contact. By speaking their name and making eye contact, our students know that they are seen. They are not invisible in our room.

3. Hand-to-hand: We connect with our students with some form of physical contact. Maybe it's a handshake, a high-5 or bumping knuckles. My wife, a kindergarten teacher, hugs her students. We make appropriate physical contact with our students as they enter the room.

We are often reluctant to do this because of news reports of inappropriate touch between teachers and students. Unfortunately, in trying to rid our schools of inappropriate touch, which we no doubt need to do, we have also thrown out appropriate touch. Hand-to-hand is making contact with our students in an appropriate physical way.

We may have students from cultures in which any touch between a teacher and student would not be appropriate. Obviously, in those cases we should respect the cultural values of our students.

4. Heart-to-heart: As our students enter our classroom, we say something that is specific to them:

- "Good morning, Joe. We missed you yesterday. I know you were sick. Glad you are feeling better."

- "Hi, Katie. You had a soccer game last night. How'd that go?"

- "Anthony, I read your paragraph. The way you used the word 'chuckle' actually made me chuckle."

You may be thinking that this is a great idea, but how can you possibly greet every student when 25 of them are coming into your room at the same time. Or you may be thinking that it's not possible to be at the door every day. That's true. There will be days when you can't be at the door. Maybe there is a student crying in the hallway or some other urgent matter that needs your attention. However, these times should be the exception rather than the rule. The solution to both of these situations is Billy. We need to teach our students how to greet classmates or other people who come into our rooms.

In every room I entered at IDEAL School, I was greeted by a student. Where do young people learn how to greet others? Unfortunately, the answer to that question is they don't…unless they work at Wal-Mart or go to IDEAL School. We can teach our students simple ways to greet others. They take on this role for a week and then pass it on to another classmate.

Depending on the age of our students and the goals of our class, 4-at-the-Door can be practiced in different ways. Before their class begins, students in a shop class at Walnut Middle School in Grand Island, Nebraska, gather in the hallway. When their teacher is ready, he goes out to them. Then, like a coach during his team's timeout, he huddles his students around him and says, "Today we're going to make birdhouses and you're going to make the best birdhouses ever. Okay, let's have everyone's hand in." As student hands come together, he yells out, "Birdhouses on 3…1-2-3." And the entire class follows with "BIRDHOUSES!!"

What a great way to establish an anticipatory set. Not only is this a fun way to introduce the purpose of the day's class, but it also creates a sense of team and belonging. Whichever way we can accomplish this, we create safety and keep the wolf from entering our classrooms. We address the human need to belong and prepare our students to become human doers.

CHAPTER ELEVEN

Results — 'Whadya Get?'

School matters. What students experience in school has a powerful effect. It affects what they think or believe, it affects their curiosity, what they develop, and what they don't develop. School is a terribly important experience because of the impact it has on students' potential, the quality of their lives, and who they become. As such, school offers us more complex questions:

- What results from our students' experience in school?
- What happens to our students during 13 years of education?
- What do our students really get by going to school?

The continuum that addresses these questions ranges from their loss of self to their discovery and development of self. As a profession, we need to struggle with these questions and better understand how we can more intentionally optimize discovery and development in our students rather than their loss of self. We need to be more purposeful in preventing our students from encountering what Red Riding Hood experienced at grandmother's house:

"Oh! Grandmother, what a terrible big mouth you have!"

"All the better to eat you with!"

Scarcely had the wolf said this, than he swallowed up Red Riding Hood.

If we are not intentional and purposeful, our students are likely to realize unintended consequences from their school experience. Although not an educator, the story of Ignaz Semmelweis is an example of unintended consequences.

Unintended Consequences

Born in 1818, Ignaz Semmelweis was a Hungarian physician known as an early pioneer of antiseptic procedures. While working in Vienna General Hospital in 1847, Semmelweis noticed a significant disparity in the mortality rates of the hospital's two maternity clinics. Whereas the average maternal mortality rate due to puerperal fever in the first clinic was about 10%, the average in the second clinic was less than 4%. Because this fact was known publicly, desperate women begged to be admitted to the second clinic. Unwilling to risk giving birth in the first clinic, some women chose to give birth in the streets.

Semmelweis observed that puerperal fever was rare among women giving street births. After closely examining the practices in the two clinics, he concluded that the only major difference was the individuals who worked there. Whereas the first clinic had been established for the training of medical students, the second clinic provided training for midwives only.

Semmelweis noticed that the doctors and medical students who worked in the first clinic also worked in the autopsy room. He realized that they carried "cadaverous particles" on their hands from the autopsy room to the maternity clinic. It was these particles that were causing the fever and high mortality rate. He believed that the mortality rate in the second clinic was lower because student midwives were not engaged in autopsies and had no contact with corpses. Consequently, he instituted a policy of using a solution of chlorinated lime for washing hands between autopsy work and the examination of maternity patients. In April of 1847 the mortality rate was 18.3%. Four months after hand washing was instituted, the mortality rate in August was 1.9%, a 90% drop. Semmelweis virtually eliminated puerperal fever from the hospital ward in 1848 when his washing protocol included all instruments coming in contact with patients in labor.

Because it was contrary to all established medical understanding at the time, Semmelweis's groundbreaking idea that cleanliness was the sole factor that made this change was largely rejected and ridiculed. Some doctors were offended at the suggestion that they should wash their hands. Harassed by the medical community in Vienna, he was dismissed from the hospital for political reasons and forced to move to Budapest. It wasn't until after his death in 1865 that Semmelweis's practice earned widespread acceptance when Louis Pasteur developed the germ theory of disease.

The doctors and medical students in Vienna General Hospital certainly had no intention of causing the death of mothers about to give birth to their children. However, because they we unaware of the impact of their common practice, they were getting results contrary to what anyone desired. Furthermore, some doctors rejected a simple practice that would have resulted in the outcomes they had been professionally trained to achieve. Today, the Semmelweis reflex is a metaphor for reflex-like rejection of new knowledge because it contradicts entrenched norms, beliefs or practices.[18]

How does this apply to our profession? Teachers in American schools certainly have no intention of causing students to disengage in learning. We have no intention of stripping our students of their curiosity. However, if these are the results we get far too frequently, we need to examine how our practices may cause unintended consequences.

I recently reread Parker Palmer's essential book for educators, *The Courage to Teach*. With the example of the Vienna General Hospital doctors in mind, several passages from his book reminded me of my own dangerous practices as a teacher that caused unintended consequences for my students. Having diagnosed my 'patients' as braindead, my dominant treatment was "to drip data bits into our students' veins, wheeling their comatose forms from one information source to the next until the prescribed course of treatment is complete, hoping they will absorb enough intellectual nutrients to maintain their vital signs until they have graduated."

This diagnosis lead "to pedagogies that deaden their brains. When we teach by dripping information into their passive forms, students who arrive in the classroom alive and well become passive consumers of knowledge and are dead on departure when they graduate. But the power of this self-fulfilling prophecy seems to elude us: we rarely consider that our students may die in the classroom because we use methods that assume they are dead."

Like the doctors threatened by Semmelweis's recommendations, I felt my defensiveness get activated by Palmer's challenging question: "Is it possible that their classroom coma is induced by classroom conditions and that once they cross the threshold into another world, they return to life?"

This question haunted me. I wished it was an unanswerable question but it was clear that it was not. After finally answering the question with a reluctant 'yes', I began to sense a renewed power within me. If I was responsible for the pedagogies and classroom conditions that were causing the coma, then I had the power to change those practices and conditions. I could make "a new diagnosis of our students' inward condition, one that is more perceptive about their needs, less defensive about our own role in their plight, and more likely to lead to creative modes of teaching."

In that renewed power came the realization that "the silent and seemingly sullen students in our classrooms are not brain-dead: they are full of fear....The silence that we face in the classroom is the silence that has always been adopted by...people who have reason to fear those in power and have learned that there is safety in not speaking.... Behind their fearful silence, our students want to find their voices, speak their voices, have their voices heard. A good teacher is one who can listen to those voices even before they are spoken—so that someday they can speak with truth and confidence."[19]

As teachers we are required to listen to many voices, voices spoken by the federal government and state departments of education, voices from district offices, union leaders and book publishing companies, voices from administrators, department heads and parents. These are all voices to which we ought to pay attention. However, in the clamor that sometimes comes from these various voices, it can seem like we are listening to the Tower of Babel. Meanwhile, in the cacophony of those voices, we can neglect two voices that need to be heard: the voice of our students and the voice within us. If we are going to be relevant and effective teachers for our students in the 21st century, we need to begin by listening to their unspoken voices and our voices within.

We need to especially listen to our students who are disengaged, not with blame or judgment, but with curiosity and compassion. Our listening will evoke in them their voice. Then we will understand them and know what they need to be engaged. Because we are teachers, we will meet their need as best we can.

Grades and Test Scores

In an effort to listen to the voices within our profession, we have asked thousands of teachers and principals why they became educators. What do they understand their mission to be? What is the value they hold that brought them into the teaching profession? Their answers are always in line with the following:

- To make a positive difference in students' lives.

- To develop the skills, talent or potential of students.

- To help children become life-long learners.

- To help students believe in themselves.

- To create possibilities for kids.

- To make learning fun and enjoyable.

- To develop responsibility in youth.

- To help students be creative and solve problems.

- To awaken students to a larger world.

- To help students see the value of differences.

- To help students appreciate language…art…music…history… literature…mathematics…science…

- To encourage students to make a difference in their world.

Not once have we heard from over 350,000 teachers or principals who have attended our training that they became educators to raise test scores. Not once have we heard them express the opposite of the dozen missions listed above. If this is what we set out to do, are we hitting the mark? Are these the results that students get after 13 years of education?

Diane Ravitch, former assistant secretary for the Department of Education, was an original supporter of No Child Left Behind. However, in her book, *The Death and Life of the Great American School System*, she questions how testing and accountability became the main levers of school reform. "What once was an effort to improve the quality of education," she writes, "turned into an accounting strategy: Measure, then punish or reward….The strategy produced fear and obedience among educators; it often generated higher test scores. But it had nothing to do with education."[20]

"Test scores became an obsession," she adds. "Many school districts invested heavily in test-preparation materials and activities. Test-taking skills and strategies took precedence over knowledge."

"Whether in low-performing districts or high-achieving ones, students were unable to write a thoughtful response to a question that asked them to present evidence from what they read. They had mastered the art of filling in the bubbles on multiple-choice tests, but they could not express themselves, particularly when a question required them to think about and explain what they had just read."[21]

Although the wolf appeared dressed in grandmother's clothes, it was still a wolf.

The strategy of measuring and then punishing and rewarding produced fear in educators because it was a means by which they were being publically compared and judged. Why do we think this same strategy will not have the same impact on our students?

One answer to this question might be what Parker Palmer refers to as "our continuing obsession with educational externals." Palmer explains this by referencing John Dewey's response when asked about the IQ test. Dewey "likened (the IQ test) to his family's preparations for taking a hog to market. In order to figure out how much to charge for the animal, his family put the hog on one end of a seesaw and piled up bricks on the other until the two balanced." The family then tried to figure out how much the bricks weighed.

Palmer extends Dewey's metaphor, "This child weighs seventy-six bricks' worth of language skills, while that one weighs eighty-three bricks." But, continues Palmer, "we still don't know how much the bricks weigh—and the kinds of bricks we use differ from one setting to another!"[22]

Test scores and grades are intended to be evaluations of student learning, but what do they really measure and what are the unintended consequences they have on students? When test scores and grades are interpreted by students to be a measure of their intelligence, that interpretation can be a roadblock to future learning. As such, these results or outcomes are opportunities for the wolf to create fear in students.

Testing and grading represent power. "(T)he question we should ask," says Palmer, "is not how we should get rid of our power but how to use it toward better ends."

In his own teaching, Palmer sought to use this power towards better ends by allowing his students to rewrite assignments as often as they liked: "I grade each version, commenting on it strengths and weaknesses. When I give a final grade, it is not an average but the grade given for the last version. In this way, I hope to show students that the intent of evaluation is to offer guidelines for learning rather than terminal judgments."[23]

We discussed in Chapter 9 how students view teachers as either judge or coach (ally). Grading will generally result in students viewing their teacher as a judge. However, Palmer's grading practice can shift that view to a coach. By doing so, the wolf is replaced by a woodsman.

During our Top 20 training sessions, we have posed these questions to thousands of teachers:

- What impact do grades have on your students?

- Do you think that grades have more of a positive impact or a negative impact?

The professional opinion of teachers is overwhelmingly clear. All but a few teachers have indicated that they believe grades have more of a negative impact on their students. **What this means is that our profession practices on a daily basis what we overwhelmingly believe is NOT in the best interest of students.** Today, like some of the doctors in Vienna General Hospital a century and a half ago, we are engaged in the Semmelweis reflex, a rejection of knowledge because it contradicts entrenched norms, beliefs or practices.

Don Batt, an English teacher at Cherry Creek Schools in Aurora, Colorado, addresses how the wolf shows up in an article titled, "How Standardized Testing Destroys Creativity and the Joy of Learning."[24]

> There is a monster waiting for your children in the spring. Its creators have fashioned it so that however children may prepare for it, they will be undone by its clever industry.
>
> The children know it's coming. They have encountered it every year since third grade, and every year it has taken parts of their souls. Not just in the spring. Everyday in class, the children are asked which answer is right although the smarter children realize that sometimes there are parts of several answers that could be right.
>
> And they sit. And they write.

Not to express their understanding of the world. Or to even form their own opinions about ideas they have read. Instead, they must dance the steps that they have been told are important: first, build your writing with a certain number of words, sentences, paragraphs; second, make sure your writing contains the words in the questions; third, begin each part with "first, second" and "third."

My wife sat with our ten-year-old grandson to write in their journals one summer afternoon, and he asked her, "What's the prompt?"

There are those who are so immersed in the sea of testing that they naively think that the monster they have created is helping children. Or maybe they just think they are helping the test publishers, who also happen to write the test books, "aligned to the standards," that are sold to schools. Those test creators live in an ocean of adult assumptions about how children use language--about how children reason. They breathe in the water of their assumptions through the gills of their biases. But the children have no gills. They drown in the seas of preconceptions.

They are bound to a board, hooded, and then immersed in lessons that make them practice battling the monster. "How much do you know!" the interrogators scream. The children, gasping for air, try to tell them in the allotted time. "Not enough!" the interrogators cry.

What do they learn? That school is torture. That learning is drudgery.

There are those who rebut these charges with platitudes of "accountability," but, just as the fast food industry co-opted nutrition and convenience in the last century, the assessment industry is co-opting our children's education now. As Albert Einstein (William Bruce Camerong) said, "Not

everything that can be counted counts, and not everything
that counts can be counted." Would that the measurement
advocates would measure the unintended consequences of
their decisions.

Our political leaders—surprise—have bent under the pressure
of businessmen wearing the masks of "rigor" and "accountability." They have sacrificed our children's joy of learning on
the altar of expediency.

Here's what should happen: teachers in their own classrooms,
using multiple performance assessments where children apply their knowledge in the context of a given task, determine
what their students know and what they need to learn, based
on standards developed by that school, district, or possibly,
state. Teachers should take students where they are and help
them progress at their own developmental rates. And good
teachers are doing that every day. Not because of standardized tests, but in spite of them.

Students' abilities can be evaluated in many, creative ways.
The idea that every student takes the same test at the same
time is nothing more than the warmed-over factory model of
education used in the 1950's, now, laughingly called "education reform." As Oscar Wilde has observed, "Conformity is
the last refuge of the unimaginative."

Are test scores and grades the puerperal fever stripping the life of students in 21st century American schools? Is what Don Batt has written
in the article the absolute truth? Probably not. But is he shedding light
on a common practice similar to the doctors and medical students at
Vienna General Hospital that is sucking the life from our students?
Batt is not the only educator who thinks so. His 'theory' seems to be
believed by a vast majority of classroom teachers who spend their
days in the presence of real students. Nonetheless, we continue to
practice that which results in unintended consequences.

"What do they learn?" Batt asks. His answer is disturbing: "That school is torture. That learning is drudgery." He adds, "every year it has taken part of their souls." This sounds dangerously similar to what Ignaz Semmelweis experienced in a 19th century maternity clinic.

Let's examine how what Batt is talking about actually impacted a fourth grade student named Macee. The following is an email that Macee's mother sent to her daughter's teacher after the teacher had a conversation with Macee about her reading test score.

> I would like to discuss the conversation you had with Macee yesterday. I have spent a considerable amount of time and effort trying to build confidence in Macee as a reader. Macee reads to me almost every night. The past couple of months she has consistently asked to keep the lights on to read in bed after we have read together for 30 minutes. Books are a part of our lives. I am an avid reader and have tried to instill through modeling and shared reading experiences the joy reading can bring to a person's life and that growth and development are the result of that joy.
>
> Now that she's had a reading assessment with you, there is a test score. To hear that a conversation took place where she learned about her poor reading test score and that she would be pulled out of class and placed in a 'slow' group to address this situation frustrates me. The only thing she knows now is that she doesn't want to go to a 'special or slow' group where she will feel stupid and where others will view her as stupid or lacking.
>
> School is supposed to be a place where we instill in our children the desire to learn and grow. I understand the need for all of you to be concerned with test scores and meeting certain standards, but at what cost? Macee was in tears this morning when I asked her about what happened yesterday. All she could come up with was that she was sad and that she felt stupid. My message to her is she is doing great, she is

choosing reading and enjoying it, and we are working collaboratively to support her in her journey. She is exactly where she is supposed to be. She is not stupid, although this is what she is feeling.

I wanted to share my thoughts with you regarding what took place and the results of that conversation. My intent is to support Macee and to establish a plan that encourages and supports her joy of learning, which includes reading.

Thank you for listening to my concerns.

Although I don't know this teacher, Macee's mother believes that her daughter's teacher has Macee's best interest at heart. The teacher does not intend to take a part of Macee's soul. Nonetheless, that is the unintended consequence that is actually taking place. If we asked this teacher why she went into teaching, she would offer something similar to the twelve missions listed on pages 144-145. She has a student who needs her to be committed to that mission.

One of my greatest teachers who stayed committed to the mission is Jim Smith, my college basketball coach at St. John's University in Minnesota. What every player on Jim's teams would tell you is that Coach Smith 'had your back' no matter what. You knew this man was on your side and would support you in every situation. Let me be clear, he also liked winning basketball games.

In the playoffs during my senior year, we had to win a game to go to the national tournament. Things weren't going our way at the beginning of the game. We were behind by six points when I drove into the free throw lane for a shot. When an opposing player slapped my arm, the ball got loose and was picked up by the other team. As I ran down the court to get back on defense, I yelled to the referee, "Aren't you going to call any fouls?" He blew his whistle and did call a foul…a technical foul on me. The biggest game of my life and I really screwed up. Hanging my head as I walked over to our bench, Coach Smith said to me, "Don't worry about that. If he hadn't called it on you, he would have called it on me." His mission was to support his players...on and off the court. He was committed to that mission.

Dave Mumma was a classmate of mine in college. We connected at a team reunion honoring Coach Smith for his 50 years of coaching at St. John's. Toward the end of the evening, Dave said to me, "There's a part of everyone in this room that wouldn't exist if it wasn't for Coach Smith. For me," Dave continued, "it's responsibility. I was pretty irresponsible when I came to college. During my freshman year, Coach put me in a position of responsibility. He believed in me. Responsibility is what he activated in me."

When a teacher or coach develops a skill or quality in a student or athlete, the young person gains more than that particular skill or quality. He also has confidence. He has a belief in himself that wouldn't be there otherwise. This confidence empowers him to deal with challenges that he will face in the future. When a student or athlete meets a woodsman like Jim Smith, the confidence he has allows him to overcome the next wolf that shows up in his life.

Are our students developing confidence in school? Winning basketball games and doing well on tests may have some value, but that value pales in comparison to a young person with confidence, a key ingredient to engagement.

I dream of the day when students are asked, "Whadya get?"

And they answer, "I got confidence."

External and Internal Motivation

Students need to know how they are doing relative to their learning. They need helpful feedback. While visiting Wendy Soderman's IDEAL School, I noticed a mirror in every classroom. When I asked her about the mirrors, Wendy said, "When students ask their teachers how they are doing, the teacher tells them to look in the mirror." When students look in the mirror, they see on their faces the joy that comes from learning. This keeps intrinsic motivation and curiosity alive.

Unfortunately, what students experience at IDEAL School is not the norm. As an educational system, we have made a decision in American schools to focus on extrinsic motivation as a primary means for getting students to do what we want them to do.

In his presentation entitled "Executive Functions: Strategies for Intervention and Teaching," Dr. Jonathan Miller, Ph.D., LP, ABPP, stated that "most often behavior management systems are based on the assumption that students...will not engage in positive behavior without external inducements." However, numerous studies over the last 40 years demonstrate that intrinsic motivation is hindered by an over-reliance on extrinsic motivation. "Adults and children alike," claimed Dr. Miller, "become less interested in activities if they are given inducements (e.g., food, stickers, points, money) to engage in the activities that they were originally willing to engage in with no inducement."

> **Extrinsic** (external) motivation refers to direction outside the person, including the promise of rewards, the threat of punishments, intimidation and coercion.
>
> **Intrinsic** (internal) motivation is an internal state or condition that drives choices and behavior.

Although external motivation may be necessary to engage reluctant students at the outset, Dr. Miller warns that over-reliance on extrinsic motivation leads to learned helplessness and dependence. "To the extent that teachers and parents believe that it is their responsibility to 'motivate the student,' the student will remain dependent on others for motivation." If the ultimate goal is student motivation, then "management systems based on principles of intrinsic motivation and self-determination should be emphasized."[25]

I firmly believe that I showed up as a wolf to my students by stripping them of their internal motivation and natural curiosity for learning. Although this was never my intention, my focus on their getting what I was teaching overshadowed the value of their desire to learn.

Star Qualities

Not only may our focus on grades and test scores demotivate students and result in the unintended consequence of disengagement, it may also neglect important qualities that students need to get from classes and co-curricular activities they experience in school.

Continuing the conversation about external and internal motivation is key in our quest to keep the wolf at bay. As teachers, we are expected to share information with our students and enable them to learn all that they can about our respective disciplines. As English teachers, we wanted our students to understand plot lines, solid writing structure, and creative thought. We needed to be able to measure their understanding and find ways for them to grow as readers and writers. However, if we pause and reflect on our original reason for becoming teachers, we are reminded that plot lines and writing skills have very little to do with why we became educators. If our primary goal is not to impart knowledge through English curriculum, then what is it?

Star Qualities are the hidden curriculum found deep within each teacher's lessons, assessments, and activities. Star Qualities are what we, as teachers, really want students to get out of our class. They are the reason we teach and what we hope develops in students throughout their time in school. Star Qualities are the character strengths that will enrich their lives and enable them to be successful in all their endeavors. A list of Star Qualities compiled by students from the Mounds View Alternative Learning Center can be found in the Appendix on page 223.

These and other qualities are the hidden curriculum in our subject areas. For English teachers, reading a novel or writing an essay are a means to develop the Star Qualities of perseverance, organization, and self-discipline in students. Math teachers use numbers and equations to develop willpower, logic, and problem-solving skills in students. Social studies teachers use historical events and world cultures to help students learn about and develop respect, acceptance, empathy and open mindedness. Science teachers use labs and the examination of the physical world to develop the Star Qualities of persistence and patience. Band instructors develop self-motivation; wrestling coaches develop commitment; drama teachers develop risk-taking.

The challenge facing teachers in American education is that the focus is often put on the external motivators of grades, standardized test scores, student tracking and so on. It is easy to lose sight of the reasons we became educators in the first place; it's easy to lose focus on the development of the life-long qualities that will enrich our students' lives forever.

Sarah Super, a trainer working with youth in our Top 20 program, reflects on her high school experience: "As a young woman, I wish I had had a gym teacher that encouraged an appreciation for moving our bodies and empowerment through being strong. Instead, it had more to do with how fast you were or if you made it to first base in softball...totally taking away from my gym experience. I was someone who walked the 'mile run' because I knew I wasn't fast. Had the teacher made it less about time and more about goal setting and persistence, my experience in gym class would have benefitted my overall development."

Regarding student disengagement, Sarah expresses that it's "not what students miss, but rather, the negative mental habits that form which they carry with them potentially for the rest of their lives. In my case, I've gone most of my life avoiding activities that require running because I'm self conscious of being slow, a judgment that developed at a young age. I drew towards things I was good at, like yoga and dance, and drew away from some things that were good for me, like running and team sports."

When we meet former students at their twentieth school reunion, would we want them to brag about how fast they ran in gym class or gush about discussing in English class Shakespeare's use of iambic pentameter, or would we rather have them relate that they've been able to hold a job and develop positive and healthy relationships because they learned how to commit and persevere? We would experience a great deal of professional satisfaction if we learned that students we had in class were drawn towards things they were good at as well as being drawn towards things that were good for them.

Yes, as educators in American schools, we pay attention to grades, test scores, and college entrance exams, but why not let our students in on the real reason they should take our classes? Sure, they'll get better at writing, solving equations or playing an instrument, but Top 20 teachers also help students develop qualities and strengths relevant for the rest of their lives.

Relevancy Yields Engagement

Students come into our classes asking the relevancy question, 'What's in it for me?' Although they may not be asking this out loud, if they don't see anything relevant, it's easy for them to disengage. If the content of our class isn't immediately relevant to our students, we can let them know that the Star Qualities they can gain from our class is what's in it for them. One way to do this is to re-name our class:

- "Welcome to perseverance class. Today we will be developing perseverance by reading Shakespeare!"

- "Welcome to courage class. You will be developing courage this semester by standing in front of your classmates and speaking about what you are learning in social studies."

- "Welcome to dealing with adversity class. Today we will be learning how to deal with adversity by trying to figure out the chemical elements that are in the test tube on your lab table."

- "Welcome to working as a team. You will develop this important quality this quarter when we play soccer and volleyball in our physical education class."

If students have a notebook for class, we might even have them write the Star Quality on the front of the notebook. Or have them put a strip of masking tape on the cover of their textbook and write the Star Quality on the tape.

156

Reminding our students of the importance of Star Qualities can be a useful strategy in combating the wolf as he creeps into students' minds with thoughts such as, "When will I ever use this 'stuff' in my real life?" Students may not see the relevancy of the content of our class, but they are likely to see the relevancy of perseverance, courage, dealing with adversity or teamwork.

Star Qualities Develop Responsibility

We certainly want our students to acquire knowledge in a number of subject areas while they are in school. However, their time in school needs to result in more than good grades and high test scores. We need to help them develop qualities that will enable them to be responsible throughout their lives.

Responsibility means that our students are 'able to respond' in ways that attain healthy and beneficial results for themselves and others. It enables them to develop a greater sense of independence.

Responsibility doesn't happen overnight. In fact, it probably only occurs in our students when they are able to develop several other Star Qualities. Two of these are being able to (1) ask for help and (2) deal with DFLIs (Don't feel like it) and Dwannas (Don't want to).

The willingness to ask for help is not a sign of weakness. Rather, it is a healthy sign of wisdom and strength because it acknowledges that we are able to accomplish more together than we can alone.

> A grandfather was walking through the woods with his grandson. They came to a place where a tree had fallen on the path. With bravado, the grandson tried to move the tree so he and his grandfather could continue on their walk. When the boy was unable to move the tree, the grandfather said, "Son, use all your strength." Trying again, the boy was still unable to move the tree. The grandfather repeated his request, "Use all your strength."

"But, grandfather," said the boy, "I am using all my strength."

"No, son," responded the old man, "you are not using all your strength. You haven't yet asked me for help."

At the beginning of our lives, we are totally **dependent**. We become more responsible as we become **independent**. However, that responsibility becomes more mature when we realize that we are **interdependent**. Our full strength comes when we draw upon the strength (talents, abilities) of others and share our strengths with them. We are stronger as a tribe than we are alone.

Opportunities for our students to gradually develop responsibility by asking for help are present in school every day. Each day our students experience not knowing something or not knowing how to do something. We need to let them know that by asking for help they are becoming more responsible. Furthermore, when they offer others help, they are helping their classmates become more responsible. By stressing the importance of asking for help, we can turn a situation often used by the wolf to create fear and feelings of not being good enough into an opportunity to develop responsibility.

Dealing with DFLIs (Don't feel like it) and Dwannas (Don't want to): How would our students answer these question?

- Would you prefer to have friends who are responsible and mature or irresponsible and immature?
- Would you rather marry someone who is responsible and mature or irresponsible and immature?
- Would you rather work with people who are responsible and mature or irresponsible and immature?

Their answers to these questions are obvious.

A major indicator of maturity and responsibility is the willingness to do what we sometimes don't feel like doing (DFLIs):

"I don't feel like getting up in the middle of the night and changing my baby's diaper, but I'll do it anyway."

"I don't feel like shoveling snow, but I'll do it anyway."

It's the willingness to do what we sometimes don't want to do (Dwannas):

"I don't wanna go to work today, but I'll go anyway."

"I don't wanna write a check for my mortgage payment, but I'll write it anyway."

Babies do what they feel like doing. That's okay as long as they are babies. However, if they are going to mature and be responsible, they need to be able to do what they don't feel like doing. Opportunities to practice and develop dealing with DFLIs and overcoming Dwannas are available to our students every day in school:

"I don't feel like going to school, but I'll go anyway."

"I don't wanna do my homework, but I'll do it anyway."

"I don't feel like asking for help, but I'll ask for help anyway."

"I don't wanna raise my hand to answer a question, but I'll raise my hand anyway."

"I don't feel like practicing my clarinet, but I'll practice anyway."

"I don't wanna listen to this presentation, but I'll listen anyway."

'Asking for help' and 'dealing with DFLIs and Dwannas' are really 'getting through life' Star Qualities. As such, they are qualities that every teacher hopes are developing in their students. Paying attention to the development of these Star Qualities can help our students become adults who can seek help when they need it and deal with those things that will invariably come up in their adult life that they will never feel like doing.

Make no mistake, our students are asking the "What's in it for me?" question, so in turn, we need to be asking ourselves what we're really teaching and what we're really developing in our students. We need to let our students in on the secret so they know that when they are experiencing situations in school where they need to ask for help or overcome DFLIs and Dwannas that they are really becoming mature and responsible.

When students ask each other, "Whadya get?" wouldn't it be wonderful if we heard them answer, "Got Star Qualities. Got responsibility.

Got something I'll use every day of my life."

Yes, we want our students to learn the content we are teaching in our class. We would like our pharmacist to have learned in chemistry class the difference between phosphorous and magnesium. We would like the pilot of our next flight to know how to land an airplane. Our goal should not be either content or Star Qualities but content and Star Qualities. Our goal is not high test scores or responsibility but high test scores and responsibility.

Negative Mental Habits

As educators responsible for the development of our students, we need to realize that if they do not develop Star Qualities, they will likely develop anti-Star Qualities or Negative Mental Habits (NMHs).

Negative Mental Habits

Self doubt	Negativity	Judgment
Anger	Apathy	Boredom
Procrastination	Sarcasm	Worry
Anxiety	Pessimism	Irresponsibility
Unreliability	Complaining	Hopelessness

Rarely do our students get stuck in neutral. Even the most apathetic, disengaged students are developing something while in school. The nature of the wolf is to prowl around school hallways and classrooms as a silent, brooding presence, ready to pounce on our students at any given chance. Concealed in Negative Mental Habits, the wolf will offer students a smorgasbord of choices that will be roadblocks to their success. By helping our students develop Star Qualities, we are providing them with tools and strategies to disempower the wolf.

Star Qualities and NMHs have a teeter-totter relationship. For example, if the Star Quality of confidence develops in a student, the NMH of self-doubt diminishes. If students develop self-motivation, they minimize procrastination; if students minimize procrastination, they increase their motivation.

Caitlyn is an example of how a student's Star Quality kept the wolf at bay. Born at 24 weeks gestation, Caitlyn weighed just over one pound. As a result, she suffered a grade 3 brain hemorrhage which almost took her life. Today, she has minimal physical and cognitive delays, which are not overt. Her challenges are in the area of executive functions: working memory, reasoning, task flexibility, problem solving, planning and execution.

Caitlyn is an amazing young girl. As a seventh grade student, she is doing exceptionally well in school. In addition, she has a profound awareness of how she and her friends are experiencing school.

During my interview with Caitlyn, I discovered that the wolf shows up for her in two major ways. First, she worries when her friends are talking about other people and saying what they shouldn't be saying. This makes her wonder if they would be talking about her when she's not around.

Second, she worries about grades. She believes that grades measure her intelligence. One day her teacher tossed the corrected assignments on the floor and the students had to find their own. Caitlyn was afraid and embarrassed that someone would see her grade. She gets frustrated when she doesn't get as good of a grade as she thinks she should. To her the grade determines how she is learning and the effort she has made.

Because Caitlyn has had to struggle in school, she has developed incredible perseverance. However, she has frequent experiences in school that result in her believing that she is not smart. For example, when other students get a better grade than she does, she interprets that as a sign that they are smart and she isn't.

I asked her if it were possible for a student to get an A and not learn anything. Maybe he already knew what the lesson or class was about. Consequently, he did well on the test, but didn't actually learn anything. She, on the other hand, may have learned quite a bit, but only got a C on the test. A sparkle in her eye indicated her inner wisdom as she realized that learning was better than not learning and that grades can be meaningless.

In our Top 20 Training sessions with teachers, we ask teachers to discuss negative mental habits that they see developing in their students. One of the most common negative mental habits teachers identify is that their students give up easily. As soon as something is difficult students often want to quit. They are reluctant to do what is hard.

Teachers frequently speak about this negative mental habit as if their students are solely responsible for it. Have we ever considered that we might be causing this willingness to disengage when things are difficult? Have we ever wondered if what students are experiencing in school results in a lack of perseverance?

As a child, Caitlyn tried some very difficult things like rolling over, crawling and walking. She struggled with these but never gave up. Would she have given up if we would have given her a grade…a D+ if she could only partially roll over, a C- if she didn't crawl like other kids her age, or an F is she fell while trying to walk? Or would these grades have motivated her to keep trying?

Because of her persistence and determination, Caitlyn is one of the most motivated students I have ever met. As teachers, we have to make sure that we don't demotivate Caitlyn and students like her by unintentionally embarrassing them or sending messages that they are not good enough or smart enough. Without those messages, Caitlyn's spirit-to-be will manifest itself in incredible ways. She will be a reminder to friends that they have the power to keep trying and to overcome adversity. Wolf beware.

If students can't outperform the 'A' students in our class, what will they do? Many will disengage. If students find our content difficult to learn, what will they do? Many will disengage. If students are not in the upper quartile of their class or on the Honor Roll, what will they do? Many will disengage. If we destroy their intrinsic motivation, what will they do? Most will disengage. But if we help them grow and develop Star Qualities, we can bring them out of the belly of the wolf. We will then hear them say, as did Red Riding Hood, "Ah, how frightened I have been! How dark it was inside the wolf." We have helped them to resurrect their spirit-to-be and restored their hope, the fuel for engagement.

Our Desired Outcome Is Success

Success is really what we want for our students and for all the adults who work in American schools. What does success mean? Although success can be defined in many ways, I prefer two definitions of success that I learned from the farming community in which I was raised and from my grandfather.

For a farmer, success means only one thing: the potential of the seeds planted in the spring becomes an abundant harvest in the fall. If we plant in the spring, but there is nothing to pick in the fall, then we haven't been successful. Success only happens when what is possible becomes a reality, when potential is realized.

Success = Development of Potential

As a young boy growing up in Illinois, I was often in the company of my grandfather. There were times when we would be driving along the Illinois River. Whenever we came to a particular bridge that crossed the river, I noticed a smile on my grandfather's face. One day I asked him, "Grampa, whenever we come to this bridge, I notice that you smile. Why is that?"

"My boy," said my grandfather in Italian, "Grampa built this bridge. Without it, people would have to drive 20 miles before they could cross the river. I also smile because I remember the men I worked with. Not only did we build a bridge together, but we enjoyed working together."

Little did I realize at such a young age that my grandfather was actually telling me the definition of success in the workplace:

Success = Great Results + Great Ride

'Great Results' means that we are getting the outcomes that we desire (a bridge). Students are learning and establishing healthy and meaningful relationships. 'Great Ride' means that we are enjoying the experience ("we enjoyed working together"). We are, for the most part, having a good time. We like going to school.

Many students in American schools are not having a Great Ride or getting Great Results. An example would be the middle school referenced above where bullying is taking place. In other schools, students may be having one GR without the other GR. They may be enjoying hanging out with their friends (Great Ride), but they are doing poorly with their classes (not Great Results). Others may be doing great in their classes (Great Results), but hate going to school (not a Great Ride). Neither of these options is true success.

If we can keep the wolf out of American schools, we have a better chance that both students and adults will enjoy Great Results while having a Great Ride. For this to happen we need to intentionally create a culture of safety.

CHAPTER TWELVE

Fostering a Classroom and

School-wide Culture of Safety and Trust

Imagine the potential in a seed. If we set the seed on a table, nothing will happen. None of the seed's potential is realized unless certain conditions exist. As soon as we plant the seed and the seed gets water, energy from the sun and nutrients from the soil, the potential in the seed begins to develop.

The same is true of human potential. Our students' and colleagues' potential requires certain conditions in order for it to flourish. Among those conditions, the most critical may be safety. Safety prevents the survive mode of our brains from overriding the thrive mode. With our thrive mode fully active, learning, discovery and growth take place. Potential explodes.

Essential to this development of safety is a culture of high trust. Within a culture of safety and high trust, our thrive mode can operate at its highest capacity. In 2002 Anthony Bryk and Barbara Schneider published a study titled *Trust in Schools: A Core Resource for Improvement*. This study indicates that the level of student achievement is correlated with the level of trust within the faculty. Students performed better in schools where their teachers trusted each other. In fact, schools reporting low levels of trust within the staff had "virtually no chance," writes the authors, "of showing improvement in either reading or mathematics."[26]

To put it simply, teacher relationships with each other impact student learning.

Culture: Our Choice

Culture can be defined in many ways. Words like 'norms' and 'values' are often included in those definitions. As norms or values get expressed in a group, they manifest different kinds of energy. For our purposes, we will think of culture as the energy that exists within a group. This simple chart illustrates this idea.

We tend to experience life in one of two ways. Every situation in our life can be considered either positive or negative.

Energy		Situation
Positive	>	Positive
Negative	>	
Positive	>	Negative
Negative	>	

Positive Situations: The sun is shining on a day we want to go fishing.

Seeing a student excited about learning.

Negative Situations: Our vacation flight is delayed due to bad weather.

Receiving an email from a dissatisfied parent.

Based on our values or desires, we tend to see every experience in life as being either positive or negative. If that's the case, the choice we have to every situation in our life is the energy we bring to it. To every positive situation, we bring either positive or negative energy. To the positive situation of the sun shining on a day we want to go fishing, we can bring either positive or negative energy.

Positive Energy: We can be grateful for the enjoyable sunny day.

Negative Energy: We can complain because the fish aren't biting.

To the positive situation of seeing a student excited about learning, we bring positive or negative energy.

Positive Energy: We congratulate a student for her persistence to learn.

Negative Energy: We neglect to recognize a student's hard work.

The same is true for every negative situation. To the negative situation of our flight being delayed due to bad weather, we bring either positive or negative energy.

Positive Energy: We use the extra time waiting for our flight to take off to read a book we've been wanting to read.

Negative Energy: We add our two cents to the negative conversation going on between the other disgruntled passengers.

To the negative situation of receiving a phone call from a dissatisfied parent, we can bring positive or negative energy.

Positive Energy: We appreciate the parent's willingness to share his concerns with us.

Negative Energy: We go to the faculty lounge and talk about the rudeness of this parent.

The culture that we experience in any particular group can be thought of as the accumulation of positive and negative energy. As such, **the culture of a school is felt by the positive and negative energy that is being expressed.** The students and staff will experience school differently if they bring a strong negative energy to school each day or if they bring a strong positive energy.

Prior to our visiting a middle school to do a presentation for students, we received the following email from a teacher:

> We have seen a steady rise in bullying over the past 3-4 years. This year, students have begun to bully teachers! We are having a very difficult time with students not respecting teachers while they are teaching lessons. Many of our staff are having difficulties with classroom management.

The culture of this school is felt. The wolf is in the building. Unless the strong negative energy that has become normal in this school is min-imized, the highly activated survive mode of students and staff will prevent learning and teaching from taking place. Although changing the school culture is not an easy task, it needs to be the primary focus if learning is to occur.

Top 20 teachers develop potential in students and colleagues by creating a safe culture. They intentionally implant four components that create the conditions for human potential to develop. These four components create safety and trust by bringing positive energy to the culture.

> "We do not need to adjust to the world; we can adjust the world."
>
> —Thomas Merton

1. Job 1: Help Others Succeed

What are adults hired to do in schools? Some are hired to teach read-ing or math, coach sports teams and drive busses. Others are hired to prepare meals, clean rooms and hallways, and check on attendance. Adults are hired to do a wide variety of jobs. Although these jobs are essential, in a Top 20 culture they're not a person's first job. Everyone in a Top 20 culture is hired to help others succeed, to help develop the potential of others so they will enjoy a Great Ride and achieve Great Results.

Our first job is to help others succeed…to help students succeed, to help colleagues succeed, to help parents succeed. Then, we are to teach reading, coach soccer, drive busses, prepare meals and clean the building.

This is the first job of students and parents as well. A student's first job is to help others succeed and then to learn reading, math, science, art, music, soccer and so on. The parents' first job is to help students succeed and to help the school staff succeed.

When helping others succeed is embedded in our culture and is the expectation and norm for what we do, we have created one of the most powerful forces on the planet: a team. Teams are rare. Many groups are called 'team,' but they are not really a team. A team does only one thing: each member helps each other succeed in accomplishing a common goal. Any group of people whose members are not helping each other succeed is not a team.

I work with people who are a team. As colleagues in Top 20 Training, we have a common goal to transform American education. Our first job is to help each other succeed in accomplishing that goal. We don't do that perfectly, but we do it well.

One of my favorite examples of helping others succeed is Jenny. Jenny was an all-state runner on her high school track and cross-country teams. Distance running was Jenny's specialty. I coached Jenny on a high school varsity basketball team. She was certainly not an all-state basketball player. In fact, if you checked our team's scorebook, you would discover that Jenny only scored six points in two years. This is because she very seldom got into the game.

Then how is it possible that her teammates would have considered Jenny to be our most valuable player? It's because she only did one thing for two years. She helped others succeed. Young athletes love to play games, but don't particularly care for conditioning drills. However, during our conditioning drills in practice, Jenny would inspire her teammates. She worked hard to be in the best condition possible. If teammates were having a hard time, Jenny would be there to encourage them. If younger players didn't know an out-of-bounds play, Jenny would offer to stay after practice and help them learn it. Everything she did for two years was to help others succeed.

Although Jenny was highly regarded by her teammates for helping others succeed, there were times when she needed others to help her succeed. This is true for all of us. We need to help each other succeed and count on others to help us succeed. When we create a culture in which we are there for others and we know that others are there for us, we are able to be more vulnerable and incredible things are possible. When our energy goes towards helping others succeed, safety and trust exist and potential explodes.

Jenny graduated from college a few years ago. I have no idea what her major was; however, as the Director of Top 20 Training, if I had to hire someone today, Jenny Docherty would get a phone call. It doesn't really matter what her major was. I know what Jenny will do. She's All-American in helping others succeed.

Is it clear to our students and colleagues that our first job is to help them succeed? If it is, the wolf knows that he doesn't have a chance. His days are numbered.

2. Communicate 'You Matter'

As teachers we communicate in many ways. We communicate verbally, nonverbally, by phone, email and text messaging. We even communicate by the things we put on the walls in our classrooms. In a Top 20 culture it's not **how** we communicate but **what** we communicate that is most important…and the most important thing we communicate is 'you matter.' We can do this in many ways.

By practicing 4-at-the-Door, we communicate 'you matter' by acknowledging the identity and uniqueness of our students. By helping others succeed, we communicate 'you matter' by supporting others in achieving what is important to them and developing their potential. One of the most powerful ways we communicate 'you matter' is by listening to understand another person. Human beings have a need to be understood. By listening we meet that need.

We communicate 'you matter' by valuing differences. Each person comes to school as a unique human being. Each has different physical characteristics, a different history and experiences, different talents, ways of learning, strengths and limitations, opinions, points of view, likes and dislikes. When we don't just tolerate, but value the uniqueness in other people, we communicate 'you matter.'

Fostering a Classroom and School-wide Culture of Safety and Trust

A man who attended our training once said, "When I come to work in the morning, I leave myself at the front door." What he meant by this was that differences in his work place were not valued. Everyone had to think and act the same way. A different opinion was not acceptable. But on a real team, it is differences that make the team strong. If we are on the same team, we need to share a common vision or mission. After that, however, the only value we offer to each other and the team is to bring something different. If everyone is like me, if everyone brings to the team only what I bring, then we are very limited. **Our differences are our strength.**

One of the most powerful examples of communicating 'you matter' occurred one January while I was visiting Chaska High School in a Minneapolis suburb. I was waiting in the main office to meet with the administrative team to plan a training that we were going to conduct for the faculty. Two sisters and their mother came into the office. After listening to the conversation they were having with the receptionist, I realized that the girls were coming from a foreign country and were transferring to Chaska High School. Imagine the anxiety these students were feeling enrolling in a large school in the middle of the year.

The receptionist asked the girls what they wanted to happen if they came to Chaska High School. The girls said that they wanted their pictures in the yearbook. "Ah," I thought, "they want to belong. They want to be a part of the school."

The receptionist responded, "Pictures for the yearbook were taken in October. But if you come to Chaska High School, I'll make sure your pictures are in the yearbook."

The girls smiled and I could immediately sense that the anxiety they had felt seemed to melt away. I suspect that their anxiety returned when they came back to school the next day. Nonetheless, they knew that down the hall in the school office there was a woman to whom they mattered.

This receptionist was not running around the school saying to students or adults, "You matter." That would really be strange. Rather, in the normal context of her work, she found a way to bring positive energy. Her simple expression that communicated 'you matter' made two scared students feel more valued and a bit safer.

When we communicate 'you matter' and create a safe culture, we meet a fundamental need of our students and colleagues who enter our schools each morning as **human beings**. In the moments when we forget that and only see our students as **human doers,** we fail to meet that need. By neglecting that **human being precedes human doing,** we threaten and minimize our students' and colleagues' ability to be engaged and successful at human doing. Human beings need to know they matter.

A former student of Kevin's recently shared an email with him:

> Thanks for making me feel like a human being in your class-
> room. You respected my feelings, validated my experience,
> and listened to my opinions. These three words—respect,
> validate, listen—are huge. Because your classroom felt like
> a safe place where my opinions mattered and my feelings
> were respected, I was able to learn. Trusting that environment
> played a huge role in my scholastic success because I felt com-
> fortable in your classroom. I was able to take bigger risks and
> think more critically because I felt safe there.

Because this student felt like he mattered, his potential was able to explode. Because Kevin's classroom was safe, it became a culture of learning for this student. Kevin made him feel like a **human being** by showing him daily that he mattered, and from that came the student's ability to be successful at **human doing**.

Is it clear to our students and colleagues that they matter to us? If it is, the wolf knows that he doesn't have a chance. His days are numbered.

3. Honor the Absent

Communicate 'You Matter' is how we want to talk about people when they are present. Honoring the Absent is how we want to talk about people when they are not present.

Honoring the Absent means that we talk about people who are not present by saying what is in their best interest. Dishonoring the Absent means that we talk about people who are not present by saying what is not in their best interest.

Honoring the Absent is one of the most powerful things we can do to create safety in our schools. When we Honor the Absent, we build trust with people who are present. They know that it is safe when they are not in our presence. They know that if we say something about them when they are not present, what we say will honor them. When we Dishonor the Absent, when we speak ill of someone who is not here, we violate trust with people who are here. Why would this happen? If we have the reputation of dishonoring others, people who are present think we will dishonor them when they are not present.

Whenever we are talking about someone who is not present, we are on 'thin ice' because what we are saying can be misconstrued by the person to whom we are speaking.

Imagine that I am saying the following to Willow about Marcie, a new teacher on our staff.

"Willow, I am so excited that Marcie has been hired. We need some new blood in our department. Marcie is going to bring some fresh ideas and make us better. Since we've been here for such a long time, I just want to do whatever we can to make her comfortable as she begins teaching at our school. If there is anything you think we can do, let me know."

Even though I am honoring Marcie who is not present, my intent can come across quite differently when Willow sees Marcie.

"Hi, Marcie. I'm Willow, one of the senior members of the department. I was just talking to Paul Bernabei, another senior member of our department. Paul seems concerned about you being hired. Because you are new, he's not so sure that this is going to work out. Anyway, if there is anything I can do to make you more comfortable as you begin your new job, just let me know."

Whenever we are talking about someone who is not present, we are on 'thin ice' because we never know how what we are saying may be translated by someone else. Based on what she heard from Willow, Marcie's not going to feel like I was honoring her.

A necessary condition for potential to explode is trust. If we are serious about developing potential, we have to be serious about creating and maintaining trust. Let's identify six ways we can Honor the Absent, ways we can build trust and bring positive energy to our culture.

Be a Problem Solver, Not a Problem Namer: The first is the difference between problem naming and problem solving. In the scenario about Marcie above, I was trying to help her feel more comfortable as she began her new job. But what if I would have addressed Willow in this fashion: "You know, Willow, this new teacher, Marcie, is enthusiastic, but just doesn't have any experience dealing with students like we have. Her classroom will be chaos in two weeks."

Does this sound like I am being a problem solver or just being a problem namer? This is definitely problem naming and it brings negative energy to our culture. When we are problem naming, we are looking for an ally. We are looking for someone to agree with us. When we are problem solving, we are looking for a solution.

Although naming a problem is part of the solution process, schools don't need people who are only problem namers. We bring no value to our workplace if we are problem namers. Our schools do need problem solvers. Why? Because we have all sorts of problems that need to be solved. If we are problem solvers, we bring a great deal of value to the workplace. In doing so, we bring a gift of positive energy to our entire culture.

Is it clear to our students and colleagues that we are a problem solver and not a problem namer? If it is, the wolf knows that he doesn't have a chance. His days are numbered.

Be a problem solver, not a problem namer.

Keep Our Lake Clean: Imagine that a lake is symbolic of your life. The second way we can Honor the Absent is by keeping our lake clean. Would you rather have your lake look like the picture on the left or the picture on the right?

In front of the first lake a sign has been put up that says 'No Dumping' and in front of the second lake a sign says 'Dump Here.' How does this happen in our interactions with each other?

Let's replay the conversation between Willow and me. I say, "You know, Willow, this new teacher, Marcie, just doesn't have any experience dealing with students like we have. Her classroom will be chaos in two weeks."

If Willow wanted to put up a No Dumping sign, she would say, "You know, Paul, if you feel that way, let's go talk to Marcie and see if we can help her with those issues before they become a problem."

I would respond with, "I have a dentist appointment. I'll see you later."

Willow is a problem solver. Next time I am looking for an ally and want to dump my garbage into someone's lake I won't go to Willow. Willow has kept her lake clean. But if Willow were to say, "You're so right, Paul. Marcie is clueless. This will never work out," she's putting up a Dump Here sign. You can be sure that I'll come back with another load of garbage to dump in her lake.

If our lake is getting polluted, we need to change the sign. Once we let people know we are problem solvers and we Honor the Absent, then our lake will stay clean.

Once our lake becomes polluted, we will pollute other peoples' lakes. Our lake has tributaries and the water from our lake flows into other lakes: those of our family, our students, and our colleagues. They will get our garbage. If we have been spewing negative energy in the faculty lounge during our lunch break, that negativity will impact our students when we get back to our classroom. However, if we Honor the Absent and keep our lake clean, we bring a gift of positive energy to everyone in our workplace.

Is it clear to our students and colleagues that we keep our lake clean with a 'No Dumping' sign? If it is, the wolf knows that he doesn't have a chance. His days are numbered.

Keep Our Lake Clean

Treat Everyone's Name as Sacred: One of the most important decisions we make in the workplace is whether or not we hold each other's name as sacred or as something we can trash whenever we desire. In a funny sort of way, we are everyone's name. In other words, as soon as one person's name is not sacred in our school, then no one's name is sacred. If we hear one person's name being dishonored in the workplace, then we know that can easily happen to us as well.

A third way to Honor the Absent is to treat everyone's name as sacred. A person's name is what identifies her. When we dishonor someone's name, we communicate 'you don't matter.' When we honor someone's name, we communicate 'you matter.'

Unfortunately, we live at a time when it is very easy to trash someone's name. It is done frequently in emails and text messages and tweets. It's become an adult form of bullying. We live in a larger culture. Let's call that Lake USA. There are lots of wonderful things about Lake USA, but regarding the sacredness of name and Honoring the Absent, Lake USA has become completely polluted.

Although trashing someone's name did not originate in the 21st century, Dishonoring the Absent seems to be the norm in our modern culture. There are numerous causes of this. Signs of this habitual dishonoring are present in three major components of American culture.

One is the shift in American humor. Today, American humor is almost always about dishonoring someone. A joke is told about the president or someone running for president, about a movie star or an athlete in the news for drunk driving or using performance-enhancing drugs, and, as America laughs, more garbage is dumped into Lake USA.

Some of us remember a time when American humor was different. Remember Lucille Ball and comedians of her era. When Lucy made fun of someone, she made fun of herself or her husband Desi. America would laugh, but people who were absent were not disrespected.

Lucy represented an era of comedians whose humor was not normally centered on Dishonoring the Absent. Our youth have never experienced this kind of humor. Unfortunately, almost all American humor today focuses on trashing people who are absent. Watch any late-night talk show and the monologue will be filled with dishonoring. Making fun of others and trashing their name is normative in current American humor…and it has been passed on to our youth. Is there any wonder why bullying is so pervasive in our schools?

American politics sends the same message. It seems like the goal of each political party is to find fault with the other. If this is the norm of the leaders of our country, how can we possibly solve the bullying problem in American schools?

Trash talking, a daily feature of American sports, is a third indication that dishonoring and disrespect have become normative. Much of this also occurs in modern American music, movies, and various reality TV shows.

This is not to suggest that this was absent 20 or 30 years ago. But then it was not the norm. Today there seems to be a norm of negativity which our students witness every day that has created a polluted lake in which they have to live.

We have presented at several national education conferences. The bullying sessions at these conferences are standing room only. With as much attention as we have given to the bullying problem over the past 15 years, it doesn't seem like we have made any strides towards solving it. We have mistakenly identified bullying as a kid problem. It is not. **Bullying is an adult problem. Bullying cannot be solved at the student level until we stop bullying at the adult level.** As long as bullying is normative in American humor, politics, sports and other cultural platforms, we will never eliminate it from our students' lives.

Each generation has a challenge. The challenge of my parents' generation was Hitler and his insane ideas. With tremendous sacrifice, that greatest generation, as identified by Tom Brokow, met their challenge.

The challenge of my generation has been racism. I remember pulling into a gas station in the summer of 1965 and seeing a drinking fountain that said 'Whites Only.' Although this challenge has not been completely met, thanks to the courage and sacrifice of those who struggled in the Civil Rights Movement, life for all racial groups in the 21st century is better than it was in the previous century.

The challenge of our students' generation is negativity. Although they did not create this problem, it will be theirs to solve. Our youth may not be able to make an immediate difference in the larger culture, but they can certainly make a difference in their school culture. Even there, however, they will need our help. We can do this by treating everyone's name as sacred. When we do, we bring the gift of positive energy to our entire school culture and model for our students how to do the same.

Is it clear to our students and colleagues that everyone's name is sacred to us? If it is, the wolf knows that he doesn't have a chance. His days are numbered.

Treat everyone's name as sacred.

Say, "I hear you" or "OK": What's going on in this picture? Gas is being poured on the fire.

How does this happen in school? When someone's name is being trashed or someone who is absent is being dishonored, we add more negativity. After I am done complaining about Marcie, Willow could add, "She's not the only one who doesn't know what she's doing. Our department head has been out to lunch for years." Willow's pouring more gas on the fire by adding more negativity.

A way that we can prevent this is to respond by saying, "I hear you" or "OK." When I complain about Marcie, Willow could respond by saying, "I hear you" or "OK" and not add more negativity. By doing so, we bring a gift to our culture.

Is it clear to our students and colleagues that we don't add more negativity when dishonoring is taking place? If it is, the wolf knows that he doesn't have a chance. His days are numbered.

Say, "I hear you" or "OK."

Before considering the fifth way we can build trust and bring positive energy to our school culture, look at this illustration. What is the first word that comes to your mind when you see this picture?

Say "Ouch": Most people think "ouch." The reason we say ouch is because we know what it feels like to be hit in the face. We say ouch because our compassion is activated. Compassion is a sign of our humanity. If we don't feel compassion when we see someone in pain, it means we are losing our humanity.

But what do we do when someone's name is being dishonored in the faculty lounge? What would my colleagues say if they heard me dishonoring Marcie? Would they say, "Ouch"? Isn't dishonoring Marcie in the faculty lounge even more painful than being hit in the face? What does it say about our humanity if we hear this and don't respond with compassion?

Why is it extremely important to respond to dishonoring statements? First, we want to keep our personal lake and our school lake clean. Second, our first job is to help others succeed. By saying "ouch," we're not just helping Marcie succeed, we're also helping Paul succeed. If I have the reputation of badmouthing people, will I be effective in our school? Absolutely not. No one will trust me. So by saying "ouch," my colleagues are helping me succeed.

If we are serious about creating a safe and trusting culture, we need to establish an agreement with others in our department or on our staff to use the word "ouch" or some other comparable word whenever someone is being dishonored. We need to realize that if we don't challenge dishonoring behavior and take serious strides to weed it out of our culture, then we are left with an unsafe culture in which student and adult potential will not develop to its fullest.

Challenging negativity and dishonoring with "ouch" or some other word is a powerful way to bring the gift of positive energy to our entire culture.

Is it clear to our students and colleagues that we will respond with compassion when they are in pain? If it is, the wolf knows that he doesn't have a chance. His days are numbered.

Say "Ouch."

Practice the 2-out-of-3 Rule: The sixth way to Honor the Absent is to practice the 2-out-of-3 Rule. In order to Dishonor the Absent, we have to do three things:

> **1.** Say someone's name.
>
> **2.** Say something negative.
>
> **3.** Say it to someone else.

If we do these three things, we are dishonoring the absent. However, if we only do two of the three, we are not dishonoring.

Let's see how that works in the example with Marcie and Willow.

Do 1 and 3: I can say someone's name (Marcie) and say it to someone else (Willow), but I can't say something negative: "Willow, I am delighted that Marcie has been hired for our department. She's going to give us some fresh ideas." By doing this, I am Honoring the Absent.

Do 2 and 3: I can say something negative and say it to someone else, but I just can't say someone's name: "Willow, I am so frustrated about someone today." She might ask me who. "Oh, it doesn't matter. I just need to vent my feelings." Isn't that amazing. Venting is sharing our emotions. We can vent without naming someone.

Do 1 and 2: I can say someone's name and say something negative, I just can't say it to someone else. I can whisper it into the drawer of my desk or yell it to a tree: "Marcie is driving me crazy!" It seems silly that we would whisper into a drawer or yell at a tree, but here's what's really ridiculous: to say something negative about someone to another person. Why? It is polluting the lake in which we all must live.

There are times, however, when we may have to do all three of these. Imagine that I am Charlie's teacher and I am meeting with four of his other teachers. My communication with them might go something like this: "I'm concerned about Charlie. I noticed that he hasn't done any homework for the past five days…and his parents didn't come to conferences. Do you have any concerns about him? Is there anything you think we can do to get Charlie back on board?"

In saying this to my colleagues, I am doing all three, but in an honoring way. Why? I am problem solving, not just problem naming. I am also doing Job 1 by trying to help Charlie succeed.

I could also communicate to my colleagues about Charlie in a dishonoring way: "Charlie hasn't done homework for five days. He just doesn't care about school. His parents don't care either. They didn't even come to conferences. Why do we let this kid in our school?" Here I am doing all three, but in a dishonoring way. I am making judgments about Charlie and his parents and only problem naming with no intent to solve a problem or help my student succeed. We have a choice. We can do all three in a way that Dishonors the Absent or we can do all three in a way that Honors the Absent.

Is it clear to our students and colleagues that we practice the 2-out-of-3 rule? If it is, the wolf knows that he doesn't have a chance. His days are numbered.

Practice the 2-out-of-3 Rule

4. See the Problem, Own the Problem: The fourth component that creates safety by bringing positive energy to the culture is 'see the problem, own the problem.' In American schools and other workplaces, people often see problems, but don't do anything about them. They attribute the problem to someone else's responsibility. This picture is a humorous example of this all too common practice in the workplace.

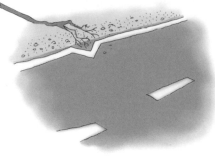

What was this person hired to do? Paint white lines on the highway, but not remove branches from the road.

A school example of this might occur when an administrator makes a decision that is not well received by parents. A teacher hears about the dissatisfaction from a disgruntled parent who she meets in the grocery store. Rather than share the problem with the administration, the teacher talks about it with colleagues in the faculty lounge. This is seeing the problem and being a problem namer.

Or maybe we notice a mess in the hallway and complain about the maintenance department for not keeping the school clean. One of the easiest things to do is see a problem and expect someone else to take care of it when someone else may not even be aware of the problem. Why not just give the maintenance department a call and inform the janitors of the mess in the hallway? See the problem and own the problem.

In a Top 20 culture when we see a problem, we do what we can to solve it. Maybe it's dealing with it directly or informing the person who has primary responsibility for it. We just can't walk by and dismiss it. Every problem in our school is in some way our problem.

> "I always wondered why somebody didn't do something about that, then I realized I was somebody."
>
> —Lily Tomlin

Imagine that we are on a football team and the quarterback fumbles the ball. What would we do immediately? Jump on the ball. Why? Because on teams when we see a problem we own it. We certainly wouldn't just watch the ball rolling on the ground and say, "There he goes again. Second time this half he's fumbled the ball. I'll bet he's only on the team because he's dating the coach's daughter." But often in the workplace when we see a problem we stand around the water cooler and talk to someone else about it.

In a Top 20 culture we have each other's back. Our job is to help each other succeed. When we see and own the problem, we build trust and bring positive energy to the entire culture. Is it clear to our students and colleagues that when we see a problem we own it? If it is, the wolf knows that he doesn't have a chance. His days are numbered.

See the Problem, Own the Problem

We began this chapter by considering the energy we bring to positive and negative situations. Our choice every day is to bring positive or negative energy. When we Help Others Succeed, when we Communicate 'You Matter,' when we Honor the Absent, and when we See and Own the Problem, we are bringing positive energy to positive situations and positive energy to negative situations. By doing this we create such a high level of trust that people feel safe. Feeling safe enables people to be vulnerable and share all that they can possibly bring to each other and the workplace. When this happens, potential explodes and we accomplish far more than we ever thought possible.

Assessing Our Culture

Let's do a quick assessment of the degree to which these four components exist in your current school culture. Rate each of the four components. If Help Others Succeed is significantly present in your culture, give it an 8, 9, or 10; if it is often present, give it a 6 or 7; if it is seldom present, give it a 4 or 5; if it is significantly absent, give it a 1,

2, or 3. Then do the same for the other three components.

8-10	Significantly present in our culture	___	Job #1: Help Others Succeed
6-7	Often present in our culture	___	Communicate 'You Matter'
4-5	Seldom present in our culture	___	Honor the Absent
1-3	Significantly absent in our culture	___	See the Problem, Own the Problem

Whenever we have done this assessment in a large group or with an entire faculty, Help Others Succeed and Communicate 'You Matter' are rated relatively high and Honor the Absent and See and Own the Problem are rated extremely low. These results have been consistent in hundreds of groups that we have assessed.

Let's drill deeper on these results. Isn't it true that if we were really Helping Others Succeed and Communicating 'You Matter' at a relatively high level, that we would also be Honoring the Absent at relatively the same level? Yet it always turns out that Honoring the Absent is extremely low. Why is that? Although we don't have any scientific research, our belief is that this occurs because Dishonoring the Absent has become such a normative and habitual way by which we communicate with each other. **We have developed a habit of negativity.**

Here's what is likely to happen with a faculty that has done this assessment and come up with these results. If the assessment is repeated two weeks later, the score for Honoring the Absent would improve. This score would improve because of awareness. A faculty aware of the problem would immediately do a better job of Honoring the Absent.

However, if the assessment is repeated four months later, the score would be very close to the original low score. Why? Because that is the faculty's habit. Awareness is important, but not sufficient to make changes. Eventually we will always perform at the level of our habit.

Is it possible to change our habit? Yes, but not just by awareness. We would have to take sustained action for our habit to change. How might we do that? Maybe we agree to say "ouch" to each other whenever dishonoring is taking place. Maybe we post the 2-out-of-3 Rule in every classroom and faculty lounge. Maybe one of our colleagues emails every staff member each week with a reminder to Honor the Absent. Maybe we do a quick assessment during our monthly faculty or department meetings. If we are doing these things repeatedly, we can change our habit.

The wolf's power is magnified in a negative culture. He thrives on negativity because he knows that negativity destroys trust and safety. Consequently, we need to pay close attention to the culture we are creating by the positive and negative energy we bring into our schools each day. We need to pay close and constant attention if we want to develop a healthier and more effective habit and a safer and more productive culture in which potential explodes and students and adults experience a Great Ride and achieve Great Results.

Is it possible to create a class where the wolf is declawed? Is it possible to create a school where students love to learn, not just in kindergarten, but for years to come? Is it possible to create a school where students keep alive their natural desire for learning?

Through our work with Top 20 Training, we have been invited into hundreds of schools across America. These include elementary, middle and high schools; public and private schools; rural, suburban, and inner city schools; charter and reservation schools. Although we have much work to do before we finally bury the wolf, the good news is that his power and the fear he generates can be minimized in American classrooms and schools. Chapters 13 and 14 highlight a class and a school where the wolf's strategies have been countered by Top 20 teachers and administrators. See page 225 in the Appendix for a special example of how an entire town is creating a safer and healthier community from the perils of the wolf.

PART 4

IT IS POSSIBLE

"It always seems impossible until it's done."

--Nelson Mandela

CHAPTER THIRTEEN

Striving for a Wolf-free Class

School and math had always been easy for Tom Cody. In the 80s and 90s he taught the top math students at Cretin-Derham Hall High School in St. Paul, Minnesota. He was convinced he was a good teacher because his smart AP Calculus students did well. He consciously or unconsciously completely dismissed low-functioning math students in his school. To Tom they were non-entities and a nuisance who were lazy and looked for excuses for not doing well in math.

Tom's experience and attitude gradually began to change in 1999 when he developed a program called *Jump Start* for 25 incoming freshmen who had a variety of academic and social obstacles in their path. In the past, students who were struggling in math were simply given more math. "This was like pouring water on drowning people," says Tom.

After experiencing more personal contact with these students and watching them deal with their struggles, he began to see them differently and realized the incredible gifts they have to offer. "They have difficulties and challenges, just like I do," comments Tom. "In some ways, it's been easy to develop meaningful relationships with these students. Because they have often been neglected in their school experiences, they are sometimes more receptive to a teacher who communicates to them that they matter. They have an acute need for someone to believe in them."

Since 2008, Tom has been teaching a pre-algebra class for about 15 low-performing math students. Each year he discovers students with a variety of factors that lead to their academic struggles: autism, dyslexia,

ADHD, bi-polar, and other serious health issues.

Each year on the first day of class, Tom asks his students when math became a major challenge for them. Most students point back to third, fourth or fifth grade when math became a problem and they began to feel that they were being left behind. They experienced shame, disappointment and the lack of support from home. They felt alone in dealing with their academic challenges and had no means to catch up. Many had gone to summer school and had failed there, too. Although math is not their only struggle in school, it is their most pronounced struggle.

Given what looked like another scenario for failure, Tom undertook the challenge of working with these students. His plan was to structure the class differently and include Top 20's social-emotional strategies as part of their daily experience.

Because these students were so disengaged from school, organization was a major problem for them. Consequently, Tom created the TIN CUP process to model appropriate and effective classroom readiness.

> **T: Textbook** on desk and open
>
> **I: In** desk on time
>
> **N: Notebook** available
>
> **C: Calculator**
>
> **U: Uniform** properly worn
>
> **P: Pencil**

Tom divided the class into three 15-minute segments. The first segment goes over homework and reinforces the previous day's lesson.

The second segment covers appropriate social-emotional lessons relative to what the students are experiencing. Tom directs this lesson to what the students need in the moment. If students are having difficulty focusing, he will do a lesson on *listening*. If students are experiencing *boredom* or *procrastination*, strategies for dealing with these problems are discussed. If students are feeling defeated, Tom will do a lesson on the *power of beliefs*. When students are expressing that they are not smart enough for math, a discussion on *multiple intelligences* ensues. Tom asks each student to share something they do well and connects that to a particular intelligence.

During this time, Tom helps his students disassociate their personal worth from their math ability. For students who could easily fall into the wolf's grasp, he protects his students from being defeated by feelings of *not good enough* and *not smart enough*.

The third segment of Tom's class returns to the curriculum where new math material is presented. His goal is still to help students raise their scores on the ACT a few points and provide them with math skills for dealing with life after school.

Because human being precedes human doing, in addition to solving math problems, Tom knows he has to help his students solve personal problems. He does this by having his students participate in Conflict Circles and develop Star Qualities.

Conflict Circles

Tom uses class time every two weeks to allow his students to deal with conflicts they are experiencing in their lives through a process called Conflict Circles. (The Conflict Circles process is described on page 224 in the Appendix.) These conflicts include family, social or school issues that students are not handling effectively because they are often dealing with them alone.

Not only does this process provide students with effective strategies for dealing with conflicts, but it also creates a high level of trust and belonging within the class. For students whose life conditions can keep the survive mode of their brain activated, trust and belonging minimize the threats they experience and provide a greater possibility for activating their thrive or learning mode.

An example of this is a student who was living in poverty and frequently coming to school without eating. Being engaged in the quadratic formula is not going to happen when a student is hungry. Understanding that human being precedes human doing, Tom's students brought food for their classmate. Their food nourished him physically, their compassion nourished him emotionally, knowing that he mattered nourished him psychologically, and belonging and being part of a team nourished him socially. In this pre-algebra class, which provides a harbor for young people searching for a place of belonging, this student's spirit-to-be had a chance to flourish and manifest itself.

As a professional math teacher, Tom has had to give up covering some of his curriculum in order to conduct a class and respond to his students in this manner. After all, standards have to be achieved. But for students who are lost, confused and defeated, standards are not going to be achieved without first addressing their basic needs.

Star Qualities

By the time Tom meets his pre-algebra students, they have developed numerous negative mental habits. They are infested with procrastination and apathy. In order to overcome these, Tom says, "We talk about Star Qualities every day. It's a slow process, but gradually we begin to see the development of persistence and perseverance. Their bringing materials to class is a victory and the beginning of organization and responsibility. For many of our students this is the first time in their life when they have been ready to learn."

A key to developing Star Qualities in students is to help them realize that they have already exhibited the qualities in other areas of their lives. Maripat, a national show horse champion, is an example. "We help her remember," says Tom, "that she showed up when it was difficult to accomplish things with her horse. She has already developed Star Qualities of perseverance and doing what she didn't feel like doing (DFLIs). Knowing that, she's able to connect those qualities that she developed with her horse in her math struggles."

One student refused to speak in class. His classmates told Tom that this boy could really sing and they frequently encouraged him. During a karaoke sing fest during a lunch period, this student turned to the person in charge and said, "I don't need the music." He took off with a soul song as his classmates went crazy with cheers and applause.

The biggest Star Quality Tom observes in these students is their willingness to get help. They come to realize that needing help doesn't mean that they are stupid; it only means that they don't get math yet.

Even though these students will always struggle with math, Tom wants them to know that they are intelligent. Although they struggle with math concepts and their logical skills are not strong, they have gifts and talents in other areas of life.

Sean had disconnected from school. In middle school, his primary concern was the shoes he was wearing and how he looked. For Sean, school was a social place to hang out. He had lost all connection with hard work and effort. His participation in Tom's pre-algebra class got him back to thinking that school was valuable. His renewed sense of purpose eventually resulted with him graduating from college.

Maria, a student who had missed several weeks of class while receiving chemotherapy treatment for cancer, emailed her classmates that she was embarrassed to return to school because she had no hair. On the day Maria returned to school, three boys brought razors to class and shaved their heads. Although their math scores are not impressive, their compassion and empathy certainly are.

Ronnie described being bullied by older students who made him sing before he was allowed to pass in the hall. A 6' 8" 320-pound classmate announced to Ronnie that the next day they would be walking the hallway together. The wolf was confronted and Ronnie never had to sing again.

Although Andrew struggled in a math class, he flourished in the Boundary Water Canoe Area of northern Minnesota. If he and Tom, with his 36 math score on the ACT, went into the woods together, only Andrew would come out alive. Tom would die from eating poisonous mushrooms. If Andrew measured his worth and purpose solely by his math and other academic scores, he would believe he isn't good enough or smart enough. However, through Tom's class and being introduced to multiple intelligences, he learned to appreciate the gifts and talents he already possessed.

The idea of the Unequal Sign that we use in our training was brought to us by Andrew. He created an Unequal Sign on cardboard and carried it in his backpack. When Tom returned tests to his pre-algebra students, Andrew held up the Unequal Sign and said to his class-mates, "Look out! Mr. Cody is passing out test scores. Remember, we're smart. We're just not very good at math."

The time spent building social-emotional strength and strategies helped these students discover their own identity and worth. They were better able to disassociate their personal worth from their math ability and empower their spirit-to-be to freely express itself.

Some of the students who take Tom's TLC or pre-algebra classes as freshmen volunteer to come back to these classes as seniors. Because of what they experienced, they want to give back. As senior mentors, they assist Tom in teaching the class and guiding the younger kids through their academic and social challenges.

Tom has discovered through his pre-algebra class that teaching stu-dents who are disengaged for whatever reason is terribly difficult and frustrating. Although it is extremely demanding work, it has also been fulfilling and exhilarating for Tom.

Referring to times in his career when he taught students in honors math classes, Tom claims he made very little difference in their educa-tion: "They came in as high performing math students and left as high performing math students. Some of the pre-algebra students entered with math percentile scores in the teens but were able to raise their scores to above 50 percentile." These students accomplished more in math by having a teacher who focused less on math and more on developing their social-emotional intelligence.

"The graduation parties for many students in my school," claims Tom, "are celebrating an achievement that was not all that difficult. But I love going to the graduation parties of my pre-algebra students because it's a celebration comparable to climbing Mount Everest."

Like the woodsman who sensed something wasn't right in Grandmother's house, Tom sensed that the wolf had done some damage to his students. Tom's risky move was to design a class to 'save' them. He accepted the challenge of dealing with the natural demands and rigor of a high school setting coupled with the needs, abilities, and struggles of the students. In order to create the culture of safety and teach social-emotional lessons while still covering curriculum, something had to give. His willingness to try something new was *not* at the expense of his students, but rather at the expense of content for the *well being* of his students. In the end, students discovered the power within themselves to overcome the wolf and make a positive difference in their lives and the lives of others.

Transforming Discouragement to Courage

Michael Cole, my dear friend and business partner, is a world-class presenter who has helped countless adults attain greater success and wellbeing in their personal and professional lives. However, Michael arrived at his own higher level of consciousness only after a long journey of suffering and transformation.

Raised in a trauma-based family system, Michael attended a high school where he experienced similar expressions of trauma as he did at home. These experiences of trauma were manifested in one class in particular. Although he now understands that school and life are about making mistakes and learning from them, that was NOT his experience as a freshman years ago in pre-algebra class.

If I did my homework wrong, I was shamed. I felt humiliated

by my teacher with comments like, 'What's wrong with you? How could you not learn this? What part of what I said didn't you understand? How many times do I have to tell you?'

I remember sitting at my kitchen table all by myself trying with all my might to figure this math stuff out and I couldn't. I was so confused and overwhelmed. It was gut wrenching to go back to class knowing that I'd be receiving more of the same. I had to go to summer school all four years in an attempt to catch up, but to no avail. It was excruciating. I tried and I got punished in spite of it. I got punished for getting it wrong.

Those early life experiences left me with the erroneous belief that something really was wrong with me. Filled with shame, I believed there was something wrong with me that was not correctable. The pain of living with shame became greater than the fear of taking actions to heal it.

At the age of 60, Michael returned to high school to take Tom's pre-algebra class, a class he had failed as a freshman. In fact, he flunked the math class he took before pre-algebra and all the math classes he took after pre-algebra.

I have been given an opportunity of a lifetime to go back to a class that I flunked and that for 45 years have carried a false belief that I am not math smart. At the age of 55, I was still having nightmares about being stuck in math and never getting out of high school. I am waking up at the age of 60 and realizing that this belief has been very self-limiting and has kept me from pursuing many things throughout my life. To my delight I find the pre-algebra class I am now taking to be interesting and inspiring. I've discovered that I am smart enough to learn a subject that I flunked.

If Michael could visit with the teacher he had 45 years ago, he would say, "Maybe some of the problem is in the way you are teaching it to me. Maybe it has to do with the anxiety I feel whenever I come into this math class. Just maybe."

As an adult, Michael realizes that when students are not learning, teachers need to have a conversation about their part in the problem.

Michael's experience in Tom's class is very different than his first encounter with pre-algebra.

> When we take a test we need to debrief the test. The real learning happens after the test. I'm not interested in what I got right. That's wonderful, but I'm interested in the part of the problems that I didn't get right. In math there's a whole series of symbols and functions. I want to have a conversation about where in the process that I missed the boat. But 45 years ago we never had that conversation.

Now when he gets confused he reminds himself, "Michael, you're learning. You will figure this out." Along with learning a bit of math, his pre-algebra experience is helping him develop the Star Quality of perseverance, "Now I persevere especially when I am freaking out because I'm not learning."

Michael recognizes that the boy he was 45 years ago is present in other fragile students in his pre-algebra class. "How do we *get* a kid who is fragile to learn?" he asked. "There are so many things we can try," he answered. "We need to teach kids to think so they can learn. We need to teach them how to communicate so they can learn. We need to teach them how to learn so they can learn."

My friend is a courageous man. It takes courage to go back to high school at the age of 60 and sit with 15-year-old students in a pre-algebra class. It takes courage to learn at any age. The discouragement that Michael encountered when he met the wolf in school 45 years ago is being trumped by the encouragement he is receiving from a Top 20 teacher and classmates who are experiencing their own journey of transformation.

CHAPTER FOURTEEN

Striving for a Wolf-free School

As I headed north from Miami on the Florida turnpike for an 80-mile drive, I wondered why I was spending a day of my vacation visiting a school. After all, I've been in hundreds of schools all over the country. What more could I learn from a visit to IDEAL Elementary and Dream Middle School (IDS). Even the name of the school made me a bit suspicious. I figured Wendy Soderman, the founder and principal of the school, must be an optimistic educational reformer who had latched onto the latest innovative idea coming from some ivory tower and was trying to carve a niche from the market of gullible parents living in Royal Palm Beach. A school tucked into a warehouse like this one was had to have a catchy name or parents would have no reason to even consider it as an option for their children.

When I came to Royal Commerce Road where the school is located, I realized that if a king had ever lived in this neighborhood, he departed a long time ago. As I parked in front of the 'warehouse,' nothing I could see appeared in any way royal. However, when I walked through the door to the school, my premature judgments were immediately swept away by the enchantment of a place created for children to learn. Everything I saw activated my curiosity and filled me with wonder. For the next three hours the learner in me felt like royalty in a place called school.

What was more exciting than what the school looked like was what I saw taking place as Wendy gave me a tour of the school and we visited classroom after classroom. Whenever I'm in a school, I'm on

196

the lookout for the disengaged kids. They're never hard to find. But in room after room at IDS, I only saw wide-eyed students engaged. Maybe, I thought, they're playing a game and the students are just having fun. Is there any learning going on in this school?

Let me be clear. IDEAL and Dream School is not perfect. Faculty and staff experience many of the same struggles that are experienced in schools throughout America. However, they are committed to a targeted, life-giving mission that is not just written in a faculty handbook or found on a plaque in the main office. Rather, the school's mission statement is a daily guide for every decision, action and lesson.

> **IDEAL and Dream School provides a challenging education where emotional and cognitive intelligences are of equal importance. IDEAL and Dream School students are passionate learners with high academic standards and strong virtues. IDEAL and Dream School models and encourages students to become optimistic thinkers, goal oriented risk takers, innovative problem solvers and dynamic leaders. IDEAL and Dream School students believe in their dreams and take action to make them a reality.**

What I witnessed was this mission statement in action and it didn't leave much room for the wolf to gain a foothold. No, the students weren't smiling and wide-eyed and engaged because they were playing a game and having fun. They were smiling and wide-eyed and engaged because they were learning.

The word 'students' appears three times in this mission statement. Students are the focus of this school and they are treated as royalty. Their being treated as royalty is not a focus on status that often results in the development of cheap entitlements. Rather, they are viewed and treated as royalty because of the fundamental worth of who they are, their unique spirit-to-be, and the power of their potential (their inner voice and dreams; what they can become and create). Because they experience their own royalty, they view and treat others in a similar fashion.

197

EQ Must Equal IQ

Key to accomplishing this and central to the mission of IDS is that **emotional and cognitive intelligences are of equal importance.** In my interview with Wendy, she began by telling me, "EQ must equal IQ. Everything we do focuses on this." In other words, human being precedes human doing.

For the first 20 minutes of each day, no attention is paid to academics. Teachers don't begin with "Let's get down to work." Rather, as my grandson experienced, they begin with, "Good morning, Joe. I'm glad you're here." Teachers establish an emotional tone of safety and belonging. They meet students at the door. They talk with their students about their hobbies and what they like. The teachers, like coaches in a locker room before a game, give the kids a pep talk. They review the day's agenda, which is written in color. The students share what they look forward to and what they need to improve on as their teachers offer encouragement.

The greeting that the students receive when they come to school is offered to others who visit their classrooms. The students are taught how to greet others with a simple handshake. Remember my encounter with Billy described on page 137: "Good morning. My name is Billy. Welcome to IDEAL School. Do you have any questions?"

Wendy and her faculty are serious about the importance of IDS's curriculum. However, as she said to me, "Meeting people is just as important." Doesn't that simple sentence make total sense? Yes, we are educating students to know information, but we also have to be helping them know how to live in a world with other people. Another way they accomplish this at IDS is by attaching curriculum or academic achievement to EQ. In conversations with students, teachers often say things like:

> "You understand fractions and you also are sensitive to the feelings of others."

> "You know how to write in complete sentences and you also have good manners."

Maintaining Intrinsic Motivation in Students

One thing I noticed during my tour is that there is a mirror in each classroom. Wendy explained that the mirrors are another way to connect emotion with IQ and with what students are experiencing each day. Teachers don't say to their students, "I'm proud of you." Rather, they will say, "You should be proud of yourself. Go look in the mirror and you'll see what that looks like." When students do, they see what proud looks like. They see themselves beaming and lighting up. Students who may have taken a risk look in the mirror to see what dealing with risk looks like. If students are having a rough day, the teacher will ask them to look in the mirror and tell the teacher what they see. This simple mirror tool results in students discovering who they are. They see on their face what they are feeling inside. They realize that they are living life from the inside out. It's not about pleasing others, a way by which the wolf tries to take control of students' lives, but pleasing themselves.

Titles and labels like 'gifted' class, 'honor roll' students, or 'valedictorian' and assemblies that celebrate perfection (the state championship team) are common in most American schools. Because these practices create an entitlement mentality of being special due to being a step ahead of someone else, they are eliminated at IDS. Consequently, the preponderance of judgment and comparison that the wolf salivates over in most schools is minimized at IDS. Rather than students being placed on a hierarchical line based on degrees of exceptionality, IDS students have a sense of belonging on a collaborative circle.

Instead of developing an entitlement mentality, IDS is developing in students an innovative mentality where process, not perfection, is celebrated. Essential to developing an innovative mentality is valuing mistakes. Whereas students in many schools experience making mistakes as doing something wrong, IDS students are encouraged to step outside their Comfort Zone and make mistakes. Because learning requires that students make mistakes, teachers at IDS model making mistakes. They magnify their mistakes and engage students in discussions about what can be learned from mistakes. "We can't be a pure environment where we need to be perfect," says Wendy. "We need room for a mess. We want our students to feel safe to make mistakes. But we're not okay with our students making habitual mistakes. That would mean that they're not learning."

Grades at IDS focus on providing students and parents with feedback on learning. The number grade that students receive indicates a percentage of mastery in their various subject areas.

The Roles of the Teacher: Mentor and Salesman

When I shared with Wendy that the primary intention of this book was to celebrate the teacher as the key person in American schools who can create a culture of learning and walk with students to help them go from fear to faith, she shared some meaningful insights relative to a teacher's role.

Teachers and staff at IDS see themselves as mentors of human beings. "We are not making a product," says Wendy, "but shaping a human being." To be effective in this role, staff members need to be consciously working on their own lives. In order to remain focused on this personal growth, staff members at IDS talk among themselves regarding their own IQ/EQ balance. They also know that as mentors they have to let go of authoritative power. They realize that their students will do what the teachers model more than what the teachers say.

The primary credentials that Wendy is looking for in hiring teachers are not available on a resume. Candidates for teaching at IDS go through a two-day audition. During this time, Wendy and her staff focus on the candidate's spirit, humanness, and interpersonal skills. They observe the candidate interacting with the students. "Engagement is the key," says Wendy. "It is my primary measure of teacher effectiveness."

Wendy wants her teachers to view themselves as salesmen who are trying to get students to buy their product (curriculum). The man who invented the first elevator found that nobody wanted to get into it. He had to go first and show that it was safe. Likewise, teachers need to sell their product not by forcing but by enchanting. Like a good salesman, teachers need to wine and dine their customers, show them what they have and why they need it or want it. To become more competent in this role, Wendy suggests that her teachers read good sales and marketing books. No salesman would want his clients to feel the need to be invisible. In the role of salesmen, teachers know what their students need and meet those needs.

My father was a salesman. As a young boy, I would go to work with him a few days each year. I noticed that when my dad visited a customer, he would walk through the aisles and write down on his order forms what he would have delivered from the warehouse. Dad would then visit with his customer about their families, fishing or how the local sports teams were doing. They never talked about products the customer might want or that dad wanted to sell. When I got older, I realized that my father was always looking out for what was in the best interest of his customers. As a result, the trust level between my father and his customers was so high that they knew he would only sell them what they needed. My dad's relationship with his customers is what made him a great salesman. Likewise, our relationship with our students is what will make us great teachers.

Staff Development

The hiring process at IDS is actually a significant aspect of staff development. Because the IDS staff works as a collaborative team, the decision to hire or not hire a candidate is determined by the group. Not only does this provide a broad perspective on each candidate, but, because the team is empowered to make important decisions for the well being of the school, individual team members are more invested in IDS's mission and operations. This is very different from what teachers commonly experience where policies or decisions are made by school boards, district offices or state departments of education and handed down to teachers who have no input. Who is better able to determine what is best for IDS customers (students and parents) than the people who are with those customers on a daily basis?

Another major aspect of staff development is participation in a neuroscience conference attended by all teachers. The purpose of attending these conferences is to learn what neuroscientists understand about learning and putting that learning into practice.

No Food for the Wolf

A central theme of this book is that the wolf is drawn to American schools because constant comparison and judgment of students result in their believing they are not good enough or smart enough. Because the wolf knows that he can't get a full meal of comparison and judgment at IDEAL Elementary and Dream Middle School, he very seldom shows up.

A second condition in our schools that makes the wolf salivate is negativity. As we've seen in chapter 12, the wolf knows he will enjoy a nine-course meal whenever negativity is offered on the menu.

As director of Top 20 Training, I have seen a shift in why we are requested to do training for individual schools, districts or conferences. That shift has been in the direction of negativity. More decision makers request training that relates to negativity in their school community (students, parents and staff). In January, 2014, we were invited to do a keynote presentation for 500 school administrators, teachers and staff at the annual National School Administration Manager conference in San Diego. Of the five keynotes presented during this 2-day conference, three were on complaining and negativity. Clearly, chronic negativity has become a major problem in American schools.

However, although he might find a few crumbs of negativity, the wolf would starve to death if he expected to feast on negativity at IDS. "I have to model being positive," said Wendy. "I have to show optimism.

If I don't do it, we're in trouble. We don't even allow 'anti' signs around the school. We have pro kindness signs but no anti bullying signs. I am the hostess of the school. Everyone is a welcomed guest. Everyone is made to feel important. When you come into this building, you are the most important part of this school." The wolf better find some other place to have lunch in Royal Palm Beach or his days are numbered.

"But, Wendy," I probed, "there must be some negativity in your school."

"Certainly," she added. "When negativity shows up, it means you made a mistake. So what can you learn from your negativity?"

She shared with me a situation in which a teacher had a melt down with a student and responded in a negative way. During her meeting with the teacher, Wendy said, "This is an opportunity to learn. What was your goal? What were you trying to achieve?" After the teacher explained her intention, Wendy said, "I'm gong to show you how to achieve your goal in a way that is more effective and more humane. It's the way we do it here to get life-long self-motivated learners." After demonstrating to the teacher how she could achieve her purpose by doing it differently, Wendy asked, "Are you willing to try this?"

If a teacher is unable to commit to a 'more effective and more humane' way, her employment at IDS is ended. If a person hired to work in a school cannot help students become life-long self-motivated learners, then she is unable to do the job. "If," according to Wendy, "we don't act on situations like this immediately, we have just lowered the bar, and the entire staff will know that we are not serious about creating a healthy and effective culture focused on the well being and learning of children."

Upon hearing this from Wendy, I recalled a teacher who had been chronically negative for 30 years and nobody said a word. I also re-membered my friend Kenny whose life may have been very different if someone would have shown his teacher a 'more effective and more humane way' than hard candy and then required the teacher to prac-tice the new way or find employment in another profession.

Results...Results...Results

The night before I wrote this chapter, my wife and I had six of our grandchildren (ages 2-10) stay overnight. As cousins they love getting together. After having pizza for dinner, the kids went into a room by themselves as Paula and I sat in the living room. After a few minutes, the kids came parading out of the room with their t-shirts or blouses rolled to just above their navels and entertained us with song and dance. Jumping up and down, they sang out, "We are the belly button family," lyrics they had just made up. As our grandchildren manifested their unique spirit-to-be, we all experienced an enchanting and magical moment.

Although experiences like this don't happen every day, they are possible. That possibility should motivate us as educators to do what we can to attain those results more often. Wendy and her staff at IDS have created a culture in which their students' spirits-to-be continues to thrive and manifest themselves in extraordinary ways. I saw it in the unusual engagement of these students in their natural desire to learn.

Since the students at IDS are engaged in both social-emotional and academic learning, we should not be surprised to see incredible results in both of these areas.

IDS is not screening students with high IQ. Nonetheless, on the Iowa Test of Basic Skills, IDS students are scoring three years ahead of average. If we are ever to raise test scores and close the achievement gap in America, we need to stop focusing on test scores and the achievement gap. Rather, we need to focus on what students need and how students learn and create a culture in which the fear that stems from continual judgment and comparison is replaced by a culture of safety and trust. It is possible. At IDS it has been done.

In addition to achieving extraordinary test scores, IDS students are reaching their potential as independent learners who are not being motivated by external rewards. They are learning how to customize any textbook to match their own individual cognitive combination.

For example, before writing an assigned essay, one student will create a storyboard while another student will write a rap song. Some will form a study group while others will work alone in the library. They know how to link their assignment to a learning strength before having to demonstrate their knowledge and understanding.

What students are learning at IDS also enhances their personal relationships. IDS students can socialize with all groups. Their collaborative experiences at IDS have resulted in their seeing value in each person. They are less likely to make judgments that exclude others. Having learned that there are many ways to learn, they know how to connect with others. They do not have a 'mine is better, yours is worse' mentality. Rather, they value differences and know that they have something to offer others and others have something to offer them. This makes them great team members.

Wendy has been told that, later in life, her students do well with interviews. As she tried to more fully understand this, she realized that their inherent desire to learn resulted in her students examining the office and surroundings of the interviewer. By doing this, they would pick up on the interviewer's interests (music, sports, family, hobbies) and strengths. Knowing where the interviewer was coming from helped them answer questions. Simply by visual observation they knew how to connect with the interviewer, how they could fit in and contribute.

Parents of IDS students are also benefitting from their children's education. Their participation in the IDS experience is resulting in their becoming **realistic optimists** in how they are raising their children.

The mother of a first grader called me to ask if I could give her any advice on how to motivate her son. As I listened to her, she told me that her son is in a Chinese immersion school and is taking classical piano lessons. He is expected to read and practice piano each day after school. In addition, her son's father wants the boy to learn how to ice skate and ski. Because he is not motivated to practice piano each night, she gives him candy after every 15 minutes of practice.

Does this mother sound like a realistic optimist? She is working hard to do what is best for her son. However, after she told me what is expected of this first grader, I said, "I'm tired just listening to what this boy has to do. I think that by his lack of motivation he may be telling you that he just needs to be. It sounds like an entire lifetime is being packed into one year. Your boy just needs to play. And rewarding him with candy when he practices piano is only going to result in him loving candy and not piano."

It's common and understandable that as parents we want certain things for our children. However, what we want and how we go about trying to achieve this in our children may, in fact, be causing the very opposite of what we want. Parents who are realistic optimists are better able to match their child's capabilities to achieve a realistic goal.

Why Do We Need School: A Student's Perspective

Virginia Tadini is a college student at New York University. As a youngster, she attended IDS from pre-school through eighth grade. In an interview I conducted with her, she shared her perspective on IDS.[27]

PB: Virginia, how would you describe IDEAL Elementary and Dream Middle School?

VT: IDS is a school that cares immensely about its students and places a tremendous importance on learning. I was there during a crucial time in my life. I learned about myself and how to relate to others. I learned academics and from books and how that would help me later in life.

It was a safe place where I could go even when I was having trouble at home. People there really cared about me. What I was doing there always seemed really meaningful, even if it was just learning colors. Because I was born in Italy, I didn't know English when I started school. I always felt safe learning at IDS. I never felt compared by teachers. There were no class rankings. Even in middle school when there was some judging going on among peers, it was great to not be judged by teachers.

PB: If you ever made a mistake, how would that be handled in school?

VT: We had a dress code at school. When I got older and tried to violate the dress code by wearing extra jewelry or make-up, teachers would talk to me in a way that helped me understand why this was a mistake. Teachers would talk to us like we were adults. They would explain the purpose of the rule. It would always make sense to me. We would never get yelled at.

PB: Was there ever a time when you felt fear in school?

VT: No.

PB: Did you ever want to be invisible?

VT: No. It was always a safe place for me. It's weird because everyone knew my life story but I never wanted to hide from that. It was nice to be recognized.

PB: Is there anything you experienced or learned at IDS that was a benefit to you in other schools or later in life?

VT: I could say a million things. The school is based on William Gardner's multiple intelligences. We learned in so many ways. I realized that I'm a visual learner. I pick up on visual cues. Knowing this has helped me with my studying needs. If my college professor lectures, I write it down and give myself visual cues. If I didn't know how I learn, I wouldn't do this and learning would be more difficult.

PB: There must have been some things in school that you weren't very interested in learning.

VT: My teachers presented things in ways that kept me interested in school. There always seemed to be a purpose to what I was learning. It mattered. It wasn't someone just barking orders at me. It wasn't about learning something for a test. We got contextual messages and real world reasons why our learning was important.

Math was my difficult subject. We would ask our teacher 'When are we ever going to use this?' Why? Why? Why? He'd tell us that it's not about knowing how to do algebra. It's that this is a hard problem. If you get used to solving difficult problems, your brain is practicing how to solve problems…any problem. He made it sound like what we were doing in math would help us in other parts of our life.

PB: Aside from academics, did you experience any social or emotional learning at IDS that has benefitted you?

VT: Every Friday we would have a school assembly that was called Heart-to-heart. Mrs. Soderman would talk about a different theme each week. Usually the talks were about the different virtues that are the foundation of our school. Heart-to-heart was like an open space where we could share about ourselves. We would talk about the virtues that were our strengths and those we needed to work on. I'm strong on determination but need to work on patience. When I got to high school, I realized how much I missed these talks.

Because of these discussions, I am much more in touch with my emotions. School is not just about studies, but being able to balance IQ and EQ. People underestimate this. I want to do something in the world and I want to do it well. In order to do that, I need a balance between EQ and academics.

PB: Any final thoughts about IDS?

VT: It was a safe place to come when home wasn't great. Everything I learned at IDS is now a strategy in my life to help me deal with problems…academic problems or social problems. Whenever there was bickering going on among us middle school girls, we were treated as mature. We'd have an open dialogue. We would talk about things and learn how to solve conflicts rather than hope they would go away. School was a supportive place where people cared about me.

Three times during our interview, Virginia describes IDS as safe. The safety that she experienced during these important formative years of her life enabled the thrive mode of her brain to activate every day in school. As a result, her natural tendency to try and be curious stayed alive. Her spirit-to-be was encouraged and celebrated.

Like Red Riding Hood, Virginia is now on her second visit to Grandmother's house. Imagine the challenges and problems she is experiencing as a college freshman in New York city. However, she comes to the Big Apple as a confident young woman aware of the power within her to learn, solve problems, create and be a positive difference for others.

In chapter 2, we asked the question, why do we need school? What is the purpose of education?

- Is it not to be engaged in learning?

- Is it not to develop a person's potential?

- Is it not to empower a person to enhance her own life?

- Is it not to develop values and skills that motivate and allow a person to make a contribution to others and society?

These are not unanswerable questions. Yes, these are the purpose of education and at IDEAL Elementary and Dream School this purpose is being met. At IDS, Top 20 teachers have created a learning culture in which students like Virginia can say with confidence:

- I am engaged in learning.

- I am developing my potential.

- I am enhancing my life.

- I am developing values and skills that make a positive contribution to others.

That's why we need school.

No wolf is keeping IDS students from wandering off the path to discover the wonders of the world and participate fully in life. Like Red Riding Hood, they have developed a confidence to express their spirit-to-be. Like Red Riding Hood, they come bearing gifts for those they meet along the way.

It is possible.

CHAPTER FIFTEEN

The Vocation of Teaching Students in 21ˢᵗ Century American Schools

The third game of the 1989 World Series was scheduled to begin at 5:35 on October 17th in San Francisco. Although thousands of fans had gathered at the ballpark and millions more were watching on TV, no pitch was thrown at Candlestick Park that day. The Loma Prieta earthquake struck 31 minutes before the game was to begin causing 42 deaths, massive damage in the San Francisco area, and delaying the World Series for ten days.

While driving to school one morning during this delay, I was listening to an interview on the radio with one of the players. Essentially the player expressed his realization that what he did for a living was really not all that important to society and that, in light of the crisis that thousands of people were experiencing, being a baseball player was insignificant.

Upon hearing his comment, I recalled the insane amount of money that players are paid for hitting, throwing or catching a ball. I certainly agreed with his assessment that playing baseball was relatively insignificant. However, in that moment it became profoundly clear to me that what teachers do for far less money is profoundly significant. Like Parker Palmer, I view teachers as "the true cultural heroes of our time. Daily they must deal with children who have been damaged by social pathologies that no one else has the will to cure. Daily they are berated by politicians, the public, and the press for their alleged inadequacies and failures. And daily they return to their classrooms, opening their hearts and minds in hopes of helping children do the same."[28]

I appreciate people who challenge our profession. One of the purposes of this book is to challenge our profession. As a profession we are at times inadequate; we have at times failed. I don't know any teacher who doesn't at times feel inadequate or realize that she has failed. Being challenged as a profession or as an individual teacher can help us improve in our craft and see things that we might not otherwise see. Nonetheless, in the midst of any challenge that might come our way, I hope no teacher ever believes that what she does for a living is not important to society. **Being a teacher is never insignificant.**

In his book, *The Courage to Teach,* Parker Palmer writes an Afterword titled "The New Professional: Education for Transformation." He identifies the new professional as one who "not only masters the core competencies of a field like teaching…(but) will also have the skill and the will to help transform the institutions in which that work is done—institutions that too often threaten our highest professional standards."[29]

Teaching is a vocational profession. It is a response to a calling. Teachers are called by the students to whom they profess. In order to do that well, we need to listen deeply to their inner voice and we need to prepare ourselves and transform the institutions to which they come in order to best meet their educational needs.

What is it that teachers profess? To profess, according to Webster, is "to confess one's faith and allegiance to."[30] The faith we confess is **in** the young people who come to our schools. We believe in them, in who they are today and in who they can become. The allegiance we confess is **to** the young people who come into our schools. We pledge to help them discover, develop, and express their unique spirit-to-be.

I am recalling a training we did in October of 2013. As 300 teachers from the Todd County School District on the Rosebud reservation in

South Dakota entered the high school gymnasium, I noticed many of them wearing dark blue shirts with the Superman S on the front. Written on the shirts was:

I am a teacher.
What's your super power?

"The lost will never be found," wrote Parker Palmer, "until they send up a flare."[31] But what if they can't? What if their fear, like Red Riding Hood's, has them trapped inside the wolf? Then they need someone who can send up a flare for them. Not in a boastful manner, but with humility and gratitude, we need to accept the responsibility of using the super power we possess as teachers to not only send up a flare but light the entire sky so none of our students are lost...or frightened.

I want to close by altering Rachel Naomi Remen's quote and offering you an invitation.

Perhaps the secret of **teaching** well is not in having all the answers but in pursuing unanswerable questions in good company."

Thank you for being good company in which we have pursued unanswerable questions. Now we can write another book together:

Why Students Engage in American Schools

And What We Have Done to Make That Happen

Here's an outline for our book, an outline that can also be used as a job description for 21st century teachers in American schools.

- We relate to our students as human beings before we expect them to be human doers.

- We believe in our students' ability to learn.

- We send messages to our students so they know they are good enough and smart enough.

- We help students learn from mistakes and failure and move outside their comfort zone.
  - We encourage mistake making.
  - We talk about mistakes and failure and lessons we have learned.
  - We celebrate mistakes and failure with our students.

- We keep stupid in the box.
  - We teach our students that stupid doesn't exist and the importance of the Equal Sign and Unequal Sign.
  - We are aware of our nonverbal responses to students.
  - We teach students to use comparison for learning.
  - We keep curiosity alive.
  - We explain the Mountain of Learning to our students.
  - We share with our students that confusion is a natural and necessary part of all learning.
  - We celebrate confusion.
  - We help students discover how they have intelligence.

- We use processes in which our students' voices and names matter.

- We create connections and a sense of belonging for our students.

- We practice 4-at-the-Door.

- We use meaningful methods for assessing learning that do not become roadblocks for students.

- We create a culture of safety and trust throughout our entire school community.
  - We stress Job 1 is to help others succeed.
  - We communicate 'you matter'.
  - We honor the absent.

- We own problems that we see.

• We help students see the relevancy in what they are learning.

• We help students develop Star Qualities and overcome Negative Mental Habits.

• We stress internal motivation over external motivation.

• We maintain that emotional and cognitive intelligence are of equal importance.

• We actively seek to grow in all areas of our teaching.

• We help parents of our students understand their role and practices for keeping children engaged.

Years after we have done these things, we will drive by the schools where we taught and a grandchild or some other significant person in our life will ask us why we are smiling. We will tell them that we loved working in those schools with other teachers who kept students engaged in learning.

Thank you for being a teacher.

MORE GOOD COMPANY

Throughout my career in education, I have been fortunate to meet numerous individuals and groups who, after asking unanswerable questions, have developed practices, strategies and materials to improve schools. In a variety of ways, they are helping students learn, teachers teach and administrators lead. They, like teachers and principals in schools each day, give me hope for our youth and American schools. I want to introduce you to a few of these difference makers and invite you to contact them if they can support you in dealing with any wolves lurking in your world.

THE MASTER TEACHER

For 45 years, THE MASTER TEACHER has been providing essential solutions to meet the professional development needs of educators. The name of the company, THE MASTER TEACHER, carries the name of the original publication Robert L. DeBruyn started when he discovered an urgent need in his first year in education. That first year, Bob saw potentially fine teachers begin with a great deal of zeal, but lose both their ideals and enthusiasm by Thanksgiving. Though all had high hopes and detailed lesson plans, they didn't have the ongoing training and specific help they needed to be successful. THE MASTER TEACHER Pd Program evolved from this need.

Now, THE MASTER TEACHER offers over 800 products and services—including online coursework, books, DVDs, other publications, awards and recognition products, and more. Over 70 percent of schools in the United States have used one or more of THE MASTER TEACHER's products or services.

All publications, as well as the vast majority of products and services, are conceptualized, created, manufactured, sold, and delivered from THE MASTER TEACHER office in Manhattan, Kansas. The content comes from educators—the people who THE MASTER TEACHER serves—and is regularly reviewed by a professional cadre of superintendents, principals, teachers, and staff associates in schools throughout the country. THE MASTER TEACHER's resources are research-based, built on best practices, and have passed the test of time.

www.masterteacher.com • 800-669-9633 • info@masterteacher.com

NATIONAL SAM INNOVATION PROJECT

The life of most school leaders is interrupt driven. The SAM process was developed to change this and increase the positive impact of principals on teaching and learning.

SAM is a professional development process using a unique set of tools to change a principal's focus from school management tasks to instructional leadership—activities directly connected to improving teaching and learning. The SAM process trains and develops a person or team of staff members who meet with the principal each day to schedule instructional leadership time, reflect on impact and develop a First Responder™ structure in the school.

SAM schools use TimeTrack™, a cloud based calendar that the principal uses like a lesson plan. The calendar tracks the time the principal spends with individual and groups of teachers and provides specific detail of the interactions.

Independent and external research has determined that principals gain the equivalent of 27 extra days of instructional leadership time in their first year using the SAM process. By the third year the gain of instructional leadership time exceeds 55 days.

Mark Shellinger, a former teacher, principal and superintendent, created the SAM process and tools with his wife, Carol Merrill. The initial pilot, funded by The Wallace Foundation, showed promising results and a positive correlation with student achievement. The Foundation supported replication, development and research for nine years. Mark now directs the National SAM Innovation Project (NSIP), a non-profit corporation providing SAM implementation and support services for more than 700 schools in seventeen states on a fee for service basis.

www.SamsConnect.com • 502-509-9774 • Mark@SamsConnect.com

QUANTUM LEARNING

It's an era of collaboration and we're all in this together to make a difference for kids. It's what drives us, gets us up every day, and inspires us to give our best. It's those moments when teachers reconnect to why they went into education and feel passionate about what's possible. It's about seeing students engaged, participating and learning joyfully. We get hooked when we see shifts in attitudes and abilities. When we know how to make a difference and see significant shifts, we hold it as a responsibility to reach as many educators and students as possible.

Quantum Learning Education has 30 years of research and experience in helping educators create positive school and district-wide cultures of personal and academic excellence. We see districts transformed when they embrace Quantum Learning through professional development and student programs. The Quantum Learning methodology is proven to elevate teachers' ability to inspire, administrators' ability to lead, and students' ability to learn by defining important distinctions about what works best. Walk into a Quantum Learning classroom and you'll experience:

- passionate and skillful teachers,
- engaged and confident learners,
- common classroom language and culture, and
- superior academic perfromance

The Quantum Learning team of passionate educators has trained more than 100,000 teachers who have impacted more than ten million students in schools across the United States. It's all about results and we're ready to partner with you to create the results you want for your school or district. We invite a conversation about your specific needs.

Development that matters.

QuantumLearning.com • 800-527-5321

MINDS THAT MATTER

Minds That Matter, Inc. provides ongoing professional development to districts and schools who are looking to take their classroom instruction to a higher level of engagement through Brain-Powered™ Strategies. This is achieved by sharing with teachers the WHY behind best practices in instructional delivery. MTM's goal is to focus on the Whole Child while building success with students so they achieve their maximum potential.

Brain-Powered™ Strategies are designed utilizing the latest brain research. Each engaging strategy is used as a formative assessment while driving higher-order thinking, creating student-centered learning, and helping teachers differentiate instruction. One strategy alone helps teachers implement much of what is on their plate into every day practice. Simplicity with high-impact! Some of theses strategies can be found in LaVonna Roth's book, *Brain-Powered Strategies to Engage All Learners*, and in her grade level series, *Brain-Powered Lessons to Engage All Learners*.

These same strategies are also shared with administrators, professional development teams, and other instructional leaders. While delivering content, teachers are able to immediately leave a meeting or workshop with takeaways to instantly implement in their classrooms. Thus, Brain-Powered™ Schools are created where ideas and successes are shared and celebrated through collaboration and support.

Customized services provided: Engaging Keynotes, Interactive Workshops, Coaching Sessions and Classroom Demonstrations.

LaVonna Roth is the Founder and CEO of Minds That Matter, Inc. She is an internationally known author, keynote speaker and consultant. Her passion is bridging neuroscience and education. These strategies are a direct result from years of research as well as classroom and consulting experiences.

MindsThatMatterInc.com • 813-360-0630 • info@mindsthatmatterinc.com

STRATEGIC LEARNING INITIATIVES

Strategic Learning Initiatives has been successfully engaged in school reform for 23 years. The leadership and staff at SLI believe that every school community has what it takes for its students to succeed: teachers who want to teach, students who want to learn, and parents and families who want to provide the best for their children. SLI helps these stakeholders transform their school by providing an experienced educational team to guide them and a rigorous methodology that is based in the most relevant systemic research.

SLI's strategy emphasizes shared leadership, professional development for teachers and administrators, a rigorous instruction process, and family engagement that foster a collaborative and trusting school culture. Its process enables stakeholders to adopt and improve on best practices, set their own goals and timetables, and dramatically improve their students' outcomes. The SLI process for school improvement ignites the abundance of talent already in the building, as opposed to focusing on deficits in the current operation.

SLI has worked closely with more than 70 low performance schools across the nation. It's transformed student scores and school culture at failing elementary and high schools in the lowest-income neighborhoods of Chicago, Los Angeles, and Baton Rouge. Recently eight of the lowest performing elementary schools in Chicago and three of the lowest performing high schools in Illinois transformed their school climate and student achievement results on state tests.

SLI is a certified Transformation Lead Partner with both the Illinois and Indiana State Boards of Education and Chicago Public Schools.

SLI schools get results that are low cost, sustainable, and quickly scalable.

www.strategiclearning.org • 312-738-0022 • jsimmons@strategiclearning.org

Top 20 Training and Educational Materials

Training: Sessions are scheduled to meet the particular needs of a school or district. Specific training is available for:

Educators: **Creating a Culture of Learning and Engaging Disengaged Students**
Creating an Effective and Healthy Workplace Culture

Students: **Becoming the Best Version of Yourself**
Kaizen Retreat: Grades 5-12; 2 hours; topics include listening in the zone, helping others succeed, eliminating negativity, celebrating confusion and making things better after messing up.

Dare to Lead: Grades 7-12; 2 hours; topics include being your true self, making and learning from mistakes and challenging negativity.
Removing Negativity from Tween/Teen Girl Culture: Grades 5-12; 1½ hours; topics include eliminating gossip, rumors and 'mean girl' behavior.

Parents: **Guiding Our Children Through Life's Challenges**

Online Training Programs for Teachers and Parents

Training Modules: include detailed facilitator's guide, videos, power point and hand-outs enabling you to conduct an outstanding Top 20 training in your own school on the following topics.

Top 20 Teachers and Students Live Above the Line
Top 20 Teachers and Students Know How to See Things Differently
Top 20 Teachers and Students Learn from Mistakes
Top 20 Teachers and Students Keep Stupid in the Box
Top 20 Teachers and Students Create a Culture of Safety

Books: *Top 20 Teachers: The Revolution in American Education*
Top 20 Teens: Discovering the Best-kept Thinking, Learning and Communicating Secrets of Successful Teenagers
Top 20 Parents: Raising Happy, Responsible and Emotionally Healthy Children

Teacher Manuals: Include detailed lesson plans for Top 20 concepts and student handouts: Grades K-6: *TLC: Thinking, Learning and Communicating*
Grades 7-12: *Top 20 Teens*

Buttons: Colorful buttons of Top 20 themes produced by special education students.

www.top20training.com • 651-308-4876 • info@top20training.com

APPENDIX

PODS: THE KEY TO TOP 20 CLASS INTERACTION

Purpose of Pods: To create a classroom atmosphere that enhances the group experience by having every student's name and voice matter while developing a sense of belonging and connection.

Process: Assign students to a four-desk unit (Pod). Questions in class are then routinely directed to these Pods. Students follow a set of guidelines in responding:

1. Each student is assigned a letter (A, B, C, D) which corresponds to a task for that day:

    A = Asker – the student who repeats the teacher's question for the Pod.

    B = First – the student who responds (or passes) first to the Pod question.

    C = Scribe – the student who writes down each Pod members' name and response; the note-taker.

    D = Voice – the student who reports back to the large group using the Scribe's notes if necessary.

Clapper – the student assigned to yell '1-2-3' or three other words to get the class to clap once in unison after each Voice gives his report. The single clap in unison creates a connection between all students and also ensures that each student is met with a similar 'applause' to alleviate the natural tension that can occur when some students receive more claps than others.

2. The tasks can rotate on a daily basis or at any interval deemed appropriate for the material: A becomes the First to respond, B is the Scribe, C is the Voice and D is the Asker. Simply rearrange the letters on a classroom chart to designate these changes.

3. The Pod members are changed every 5-7 class days to ensure that the students interact with a wide variety of classmates.

4. Pod rules include: A. Everyone gets to answer every question.

                             B. Respect is shown to the speaker:
                                  • No side conversations
                                  • Face (turn shoulders towards) the person who is speaking
                                  • Use good non-verbals
                             C. No inter-podding or talking to students in another Pod.

D. No Pod ripping by complaining about or disrespecting Pod members.

5. Teacher Tips:

A. Listen closely to student's personal answers to Pod questions.

B. Pods can be used in all content areas.

C. Make a sign of the letters and tasks: Attach the letters to the sign by velcro so they can be easily moved.

STAR QUALITIES

Personal Star Qualities:
Self-confident: believing in my self and my abilities
Risk-taking: taking the difficult road to expand my comfort zone
Self-motivated: getting myself started
Enthusiastic: having energy and interest for what I'm doing
Reflective: truly looking at myself
Emotionally aware: in touch with how my feelings influence my actions
Empowered: realizing that I'm in charge of my future
Responsible: being dependable; someone others can count on
Self-disciplined: taking control of myself
Flexible: adapting to change and the stress created by it
Tough: dealing with adversity when things aren't going my way
Courageous: responding in spite of fear or lack of confidence
Committed: valuing putting forth my full effort
Optimistic: hopeful, valuing the positive
Opportunistic: keeping my eyes and ears open for possibilities; seeing problems as learning opportunities

Social Star Qualities:
Fun: realizing that learning and working with others can be joyful
Respectful: honoring others by my words and actions
Accepting: valuing diversity and people who are different from me
Engaging: willing to listen to others and share appropriately
Honest: valuing living with truth and communicating truth
Empathetic: understanding what others are going through
Team player: helping; working well with others
Open minded: accepting points of view different than my own
Tactful: expressing myself with concern for other's feelings
Kind: going out of my way to be nice and considerate of others

Problem Solving Star Qualities:
Resolving Conflict: working through issues in a peaceful manner
Managing Time: making good use of my time
Proactive: seeing what needs to be done and doing it
Focused: keeping my attention on the task or goal
Persistent: sticking with the job until it is finished
Patient: realizing that success often doesn't come easily
Organized: planning how to look ahead and keep my life in order
Setting Goals: planning to meet long and short-term needs
Creative: inventing by seeing and doing things in a new way
Resourceful: finding a way to get the job done

Special 'Getting-through-life' Star Qualities:
Asking for Help
Dealing with DFLIs (Don't feel like it) and Dwannas (Don't want to)

CONFLICT CIRCLES

The room is set up in one large circle or two concentric circles if space dictates. The ground rules for this process are then carefully explained:

1. Confidentiality: Students are asked to commit to keeping the information shared to themselves. (Note: As always, teachers are bound to report anything that could be physically or emotionally harmful to any student. Share this with your students whenever you do Conflict Circles.)

2. Respect: It is vital that student conduct is respectful during this process. Students are asked to sit up, face the speaker and listen with respect. No side talking is allowed during this time.

3. Add any other ground rules the students suggest.

The process begins by having one student volunteer to share a personal issue, a real-life conflict, concern or problem. The severity of these issues varies greatly from the simple ("My brother uses my things without asking me.") to the complex ("My step-mother ignores me."). After the conflict is shared, the following five steps are followed:

1. Two students are asked to briefly **rephrase the conflict**. The person sharing the conflict calls on volunteers who direct the rephrase back to him or her. Students are encouraged to use feeling words in this step: Examples: "I hear frustration and anger in your statement."
    "You sound sad about that."

2. **Clarifying questions are asked**. Students with questions raise their hand and are called upon by the person sharing the conflict. No direct advice or feedback is allowed at this point.

   Examples: "How long has this been going on?"
                "What don't your parents like about your friend?"

3. Once the questions have clarified the situation, **direct feedback and advice is given**. Students who want to offer something raise their hands and the person sharing the conflict calls upon them.

   Examples: "I'd talk to your coach about this problem after practice."
                "When I ran into an issue like this, I realized I needed to ask my parents for help."

4. **A commitment is made**. The person sharing the conflict tells the group what she is willing to do.

   Example: "I will talk to my science teacher about this problem."

5. The final step involves **take-aways**. The other students are asked to share any insights or ideas they might have had during the Conflict Circle process.

   Example: "I realize that if we don't listen well that we create a misunderstanding."

Note: Usually two or three conflicts can be covered during a 45-minute class period.

STRIVING FOR A WOLF-FREE COMMUNITY

Fairmont: Pursuing the Positive -- Our Journey and Our Future

Nestled in the southwest corner of Minnesota, Fairmont is a community of 10,500 people. In the summer of 2012, I received a phone call from Greg Brolsma, the police chief in Fairmont. He was aware that during the previous year we had provided Top 20 training for the faculty of the local school district. Greg's concern was for the youth of his community and the challenges they were experiencing from the wolves they were meeting in and out of school. His goal was to create an entire community that would protect youth from these threats.

His call was to determine how everyone in Fairmont could learn and practice Top 20 principles.

Leadership Takes Action

Prior to the chief's call, Fairmont leaders were actively searching for ways to develop the potential of youth and their entire community. The Healthy Youth Committee, founded on Search Institute's 40 Developmental Assets, was using results from a recent survey to identify ways to raise assets in youth. Committee members knew that Top 20 concepts, adopted and practiced by both kids and adults, was one of the best ways to raise those assets. At the same time, the Fairmont Chamber of Commerce was searching for ways to help Fairmont be a more positive community. Aware that Top 20 Training's work throughout the country in creating safety and trust in school and business cultures, the Healthy Youth Committee and Chamber of Commerce partnered in an effort to accomplish these goals.

Following a few initial meetings with members of the Healthy Youth Committee, the Chamber of Commerce, the school district and Top 20 Training, a plan was established to deal with the wolf's presence in Fairmont. The first step was to train as many residents as possible on several key Top 20 concepts. Within the first year, about 2,700 Fairmont people experienced Top 20 training in a variety of settings: all middle school and high school students were trained at school, parents were trained during evening sessions, and day sessions trained over 500 area business owners and their employees. In addition, special sessions were hosted for senior citizens, coaches and mentors, and members of the faith community.

The primary focus of the adult training centered on four key concepts: Helping Others Succeed, Communicating 'You Matter', Honoring the Absent, and See and Own the Problem. Leaders of the Top 20 project decided to focus on each of these concepts for three months each year.

- September-October = Help Others Succeed

- November-January = Communicate 'You Matter'

- February-March = Honor the Absent

- April-May = See the Problem, Own the Problem

Top 20 Champions of Action

One of the amazing results of the initial trainings is the identification of 120 Champions, local folks who are volunteering to keep the four key Top 20 concepts alive in the Fairmont community. They have promoted and conducted a wide variety of ongoing actions to further imbed the Top 20 concepts in youth and adults. Some of these include:

- A semester course on additional Top 20 concepts for all 7th graders

- Piloting of a Top 20 curriculum in 1st through 6th grade

- Community members visiting the high school homerooms throughout the year to share ways of living Top 20 concepts

- Articles written weekly in the local newspaper and sent to 120 Top 20 Champions

- Development of a Fairmont Area Top 20 Facebook page

- Purchasing and providing Top 20 online training tools for businesses

- Conducting a Top 20 book study for early childhood parents

- Meetings with executives of Top 20 trained companies

- Highlighting Top 20 concepts on signs in front of local stores

- Celebrating Fairmont as a Top 20 town during the community's summer festival and parade

- Providing additional training and development of Top 20 concepts for businesses by local Presentation College

- Creating a mission statement, tagline and logo to guide ongoing efforts

What a Difference You've Made in My Life

Although only in its second year, the efforts made by the leaders, Champions and residents of this small community are bearing fruit. Examples of the difference these people have made for their youth and each other include:

- A band teacher complimenting the band for a banner year using Top 20 principles.

- A parent who appreciated the positive outcomes after learning and practicing a 'do-over'.

- A high school student, upset about her basketball playing time, telling her parents she will stay 'Above the Line'.

- An executive sharing the successful use of 'The Frame' after a corporate meeting that had gone poorly.

- A community person calling the writer of Top 20 newspaper articles to express how much the articles mean to her.

- A grade school student using 'The Frame' to help her with a problem she had on the playground.

- A first grade teacher who credits the habits of Top 20 with promoting a positive classroom climate.

- An EBD student who used 'Keep Your Day' to help him get along with others.

- A city council person who wants banners in the community about Fairmont being the first Top 20 community.

Some months into Fairmont's effort to create a safer and healthier community, I received an email from Joe Brown, superintendent of schools. Joe shared meeting an elderly member of the community who said to him, "I'm noticing that people in Fairmont don't talk about each other much anymore."

The wolf is on the run. He knows that there's a police chief and too many wise grandmothers and woodsmen in Fairmont that are preventing him from snatching up their youth. He's decided to try other communities where he stands a better chance of being successful.

ENDNOTES

INTRODUCTION

[1] Palmer, Parker. (2007). *The Courage to Teach*. San Francisco: Josey-Bass, p. 2.

[2] Robinson, Ken. (2011). *Out of Our Minds*. Chichester, United Kingdom: Capstone Publishing Ltd, p. 71-72.

[3] See: Crotty, James M. "Motivation Matters: 40% Of High School Students Chronically Disengaged From School," (March 13, 2013). http://www.forbes.com/sites/jamesmarshallcrotty/2013/03/13/motivation-matters-40-of-high-school-students-chronically-disengaged-from-school/ (retrieved May 2014).

[4] Robinson, K. p. 226.

PART 1: A PLACE CALLED SCHOOL

[1] See: Brothers Grimm. Little Red Riding Hood. http://www.eastoftheweb.com/short-stories/UBooks/LittRed.shtml (retrieved May 2014)

[2] Robinson, K. p. 7-8.

[3] Webster's Third New International Dictionary, Philip Babcock Gove, editor. Springfield, MA, p. 723.

[4] Robinson, K. p. 179.

[5] Ibid. p. 16.

[6] Ibid. p. 59.

[7] Ibid. p. 122.

[8] Palmer, P. p. 21, 29.

[9] Ibid. p. 21.

[10] Robinson, K. p. 62-63.

[11] Brown, Brene'. (2012). *Daring Greatly*, New York: Gotham Books, p. 26.

[12] Ibid. p. 76.

[13] Dyer, Wayne. (2012). *Wishes Fulfilled*. New York: Hay House.

[14] Robinson, K. p. 85.

[15] Ibid. p. 102-103.

[16] Brown, B. p. 16.

PART 2: THE INNER LIFE OF STUDENTS

[1] Brown, B. p. 61.

[2] Robinson, K. p. 66.

[3] DePorter, Bobbi, Reardon, Mark, and Singer-Nourie, Sarah. (1999). *Quantum Teaching: Orchestrating Student Success*. Boston: Allyn and Bacon, p. 19-20.

[4] Caine, Renate Nummela and Caine, Geoffrey. (1997). *Education on the Edge of Possibility*. Alexandria, Virginia: Association for Supervision and Curriculum Development, p. 124.

[5] Robinson, K. p. 154.

[6] For more of Rachel Stafford's heartfelt stories and wisdom for parenting, visit http://www.handsfreemama.com.

[7] See: The History Place presents A. Lincoln. http://www.historyplace.com/lincoln/ (retrieved May 2014).

[8] See: Perez-Pena, Richard. "Chronically Absent' Students Skew School Data, Study Finds, Citing Parents' Role," (May 17, 2012). http://www.nytimes.com/2012/05/17/education/up-to-15-percent-of-students-chronically-skip-school-johns-hopkins-finds.html?_r=0 (retrieved May 2014).

[9] Chopra, Deepak and Tanzi, Rudolph. (2012). *Super Brain*. New York: Harmony Books. p. 32-33.

[10] Robinson, K. p. 102-103.

[11] Ibid. p. 109, 119.

[12] Gardner, Howard. (1983). *Frames of Mind: The Theory of Multiple Intelligences*. New York: Basic Books.

[13] Robinson, K. p. 123-125.

PART 3: ENGAGEMENT 101

[1] Parker, P. p. 36-37.

[2] See: Nadja Salerno-Sonnenberg. http://www.nadjasalernosonnenberg.com (retrieved May 2014).

[3] See: Lauryn Williams. http://lauryn-williams.com/ (retrieved May 2014).

[4] Ginott, Haim G. (1972) *Teacher and child: A Book for Parents and Teachers*. New York: The MacMillan Company, p. 15.

[5] See: Ignaz Philipp Semelweis. http://www.britannica.com/EBchecked/top-

ic/534198/Ignaz-Philipp-Semmelweis and http://www.historylearningsite. co.uk/ignaz_semmelweis.htm (retrieved May 2014).

[6] Palmer, P. p. 42-47.

[7] Ravitch, Diane. (2010). *The Death and Life of the Great American School System.* New York: Basic Books, p. 16.

[8] Ibid. p. 107-108.

[9] Palmer, P. p. xiii-xiv.

[10] Ibid. p. 141-142.

[11] See: Don Batt. How Standardized Testing Destroys Creativity and the Joy of Learning," (March 10, 2013). http://www.denverpost.com/ci_22742832/monster-spring (retrieved May 2014).

[12] Dr. Jonathan Miller, Ph.D., LP, ABPP,D "Executive Functions: Strategies for Intervention and Teaching," presentation on June 11, 2013.

[13] Catherine Gewertz, "'Trusting' School Community Linked to Student Gains," *Education Week*, Oct. 16, 2002. p. 8.

PART 4: IT IS POSSIBLE

[1] Tadini, Virginia. Personal Interview. January 11, 2014.

[2] Palmer, P. p. xii.

[3] Ibid. p. xviii.

[4] Webster's Third New International Dictionary, Philip Babcock Gove, editor. Springfield, MA. p. 1811.

[5] Palmer, P. p. 181.